Applied Program Evaluation
in Local Government

Applied Program Evaluation in Local Government

Theodore H. Poister
James C. McDavid
Anne Hoagland Magoun
The Pennsylvania State University

LexingtonBooks
D.C. Heath and Company
Lexington, Massachusetts
Toronto

Library of Congress Cataloging in Publication Data

Poister, Theodore H.
Applied program evaluation in local government.

Includes index.
1. Municipal services—Evaluation—Case studies. 2. Williamsport,
Pa.—Transit systems. 3. Housing rehabilitation—Pennsylvania—Harrisburg.
4. Crime prevention—Pennsylvania—York. I. McDavid, James C., joint
author. II. Magoun, Anne H., joint author. III. Title.
HD4431.P65   363.5   78-20374
ISBN 0-669-02731-6

Copyright © 1979 by D.C. Heath and Company

Published simultaneously in Canada.

Printed in the United States of America.

International Standard Book Number: 0-669-02731-6

Library of Congress Catalog Card Number: 78-20374

To our families,
who make it all
worthwhile.

Molly
Chantal
Jonathan
(THP)

Barbara
Kristi
(JCM)

Peter
Steven
(AHM)

Contents

List of Figures

List of Tables

Preface

This book grows out of the authors' experience in working with small and medium-size cities in Pennsylvania in the evaluation of the effectiveness of various public programs. The primary purpose of this work was to provide local decision makers with information which they can use to improve program performance in the future. Second, we were interested in helping cities develop stronger data-collection and analytical abilities so that they can conduct more of this kind of work on an inhouse basis. The particular evaluations reported in this book were conducted by university researchers in conjunction with city officials, utilizing relatively low-level, low-cost research approaches which are particularly appropriate for small and medium-size cities. On the basis of this experience, we have become convinced that such low-level evaluations are feasible in these types of cities and that, applied on a selective basis, they can produce worthwhile information which will be fed into the decision-making process.

One of the three case studies used to illustrate the approach presented in this book concerns the public transit system in Williamsport, Pennsylvania, and was conducted as a private consulting project in collaboration with city officials. The Lycoming County Planning Commission is to be thanked for its permission to include these materials in the book. The other two case studies, involving a housing-rehabilitation program in Harrisburg, Pennsylvania, and a crime-prevention program in York, Pennsylvania, were conducted as part of a larger research/continuing education project of the Institute of Public Administration at The Pennsylvania State University. This project, funded by the U.S. Office of Education, gave us an opportunity to test our ideas about the feasibility of program evaluation in such cities. We would like to further acknowledge the institutional support provided by Robert J. Mowitz, Director of the Institute, for completing the follow-up work necessary to put this material into book form. We would also like to thank two research assistants who worked for the Institute in earlier stages of these projects, Charles DeBrunner and William Reemsten.

Officials in all three cities who were connected with the programs being evaluated gave their full support and cooperation in terms of ensuring access to data and in providing generous staff support. The principal individuals involved in Harrisburg included Wilmer Faust, Director of the Bureau of Planning; Dorothy Friedman and Seung Chon, staff planners; and Allie Harper, Director of Codes Enforcement. Their commitment to the housing-rehabilitation program and their openminded approach toward evaluating its performance were highly conducive to a formative evaluation. In York the architects of the crime-prevention program were James E. Hooker, Director of Public Safety; and Donald Murphy, Police Planner.

Their willingness to commit staff resources to the evaluation and their frank interactions in terms of interpreting results made for a particularly healthy working relationship. In Williamsport, Thomas Spitler, Director of Personnel and Finance; Joseph Zavisca, former manager of the Bureau of Transportation; and William Nichols, present manager of the Bureau of Transportation, all played major roles in getting the data collected and the analytical work completed. Their concern for linking planning and evaluation to implementation resulted in a study which led directly to improved service delivery. We are grateful for the enthusiastic support of all these individuals.

Finally, we are indebted to a number of people at the Institute of Public Administration who helped in completing the manuscript. We were extremely fortunate to have the able and willing assistance of four graduate assistants in actually putting the book together: Cindi Downing, Scott Huebner, Cindy Rhodes, and Rick Thompson. In addition, the competent typing and cheerful assistance of Debbie Putt and Nancy Dietrich made manuscript production a painless process.

University Park   *Theodore H. Poister*
Fall, 1978   *James C. McDavid*
                                        Anne Hoagland Magoun

1

Evaluating Program Performance

Introduction

This book is concerned with evaluating the performance of local governmental programs and projects, particularly in small and medium-size cities. It draws on the experience of university researchers working as consultants with officials in three Pennsylvania cities on evaluation efforts and is based on the premise that the research approach and the results of these projects will be instructive to students as well as to practitioners who may be presently involved with program evaluation or contemplating the worth of undertaking evaluations in the future. While the actual evaluations discussed here were conducted with the purpose of examining the effectiveness of a housing-rehabilitation program, a crime-prevention program, and a mass-transit-improvement program, in particular, this book is concerned primarily with the broader utility of the evaluation procedures illustrated.

Program evaluation in general is a growing area in the field of public administration as the expanding literature will attest.[1] This growth can be viewed as part of a larger trend toward the development and adaptation of improved management technology in the public sector which has accelerated in recent years due primarily to the financial difficulties experienced by many governmental units and the general recognition that government must operate within a framework of more limiting financial constraints than in previous periods. The resulting heightened concern with increasing the effectiveness, efficiency, and accountability of government and the delivery of public services has spawned greater interest in program evaluation, along with such managerial techniques as program and zero-based budgeting, cost accounting, management by objectives, management information systems, management-incentive programs, and productivity-review programs. In addition, the growing awareness that many new social programs focusing principally on so-called urban problems are of questionable value in alleviating the conditions they were designed to address has led to increased interest in evaluation research in particular.

The primary impetus for the increasing activity in the area of evaluation has come at the federal and state levels, while local jurisdictions have been slower to build evaluation into their planning and programming processes on a systematic basis. There is, however, a growing trend toward evaluation in city governments as they become more aware of its potential and develop

1

the staff capabilities necessary to undertake the work, and more particularly, as they are required to include evaluations as part of federal- and state-sponsored grant programs. While much of the literature would appear to indicate a lack of program evaluation at the local level,[2] indications are that this kind of activity is on the increase. Of those jurisdictions responding to a 1976 survey conducted by the International City Management Association, 62 percent of the cities with 50,000 to 100,000 population reported some experience with program evaluation.[3]

Especially in small and medium-size cities, with their more limited resources and staff capabilities, these trends raise important questions about (1) their ability to undertake sound evaluations, at least on an inhouse basis, (2) the direct costs involved, and (3) the usefulness of the evaluations in the first place, that is, the worth of the results they produce to decision makers. This book cannot provide definitive answers to these questions. However, it is predicated on the assumption that program evaluation is a feasible and worthwhile enterprise for smaller cities, as well as for larger jurisdictions, which can produce important information about program performance. These three underlying issues of feasibility, cost, and usefulness are analyzed in the concluding chapter in the context of the three case illustrations.

Purpose

This book presents an approach to program-performance evaluation for local government which is particularly suitable for smaller jurisdictions. Intended for both students and professionals in the field, it has two basic objectives: (1) to provide methodological guidelines for city planners and other staff analysts involved in the conduct of evaluations, and (2) to generate increased awareness and interest in evaluation on the part of program managers and policy makers. In general, its objective is to illustrate the potential role of program evaluation in local government as well as to show how worthwhile evaluations can be designed and carried out.

The evaluation approach which is the core of this book is presented first through a general discussion of the research issues and procedures involved and is then illustrated through its application to the three specific program evaluations mentioned previously. This book is not intended to serve as a single-source, "how to do it" manual for potential program evaluators,[4] and the reader should not be misled into thinking that other program evaluations could be conducted as precise repetitions of the case studies included here. Indeed, each individual program, taken together with its operating context, presents the evaluator with a unique set of opportunities and constraints, as is made clear by a comparison of these cases.

The case studies covered here for the most part require little indepth statistical analysis, although in some instances more advanced statistical techniques are applied in order to elaborate interpretations of the data. Given some degree of staff background and training in general research and data-collection methods, similar evaluations are feasible on an inhouse basis in small cities, with reference to standard texts and sources. Alternatively, city staffs could take the major responsibility for conducting evaluations and call on outside consultants for assistance in establishing the research design and providing guidance for the data analysis.

The approach to evaluation outlined here is not unique to this book nor to the case studies presented. What is worthwhile about it is that it provides a framework for conducting fairly selective, targeted types of evaluation that can produce valid results and yet be "doable" in small and medium-size cities. It represents the adaptation and application of existing research methods to a particular context rather than the development of new management or research technology. The basic attractiveness of this approach for smaller cities is the fact that it attempts to provide usable information concerning the central issues of program performance at relatively low cost.

Evaluating Program Effectiveness

Any systematic procedure for evaluating the performance of a public program will necessarily involve specifying criteria on which the evaluation is to be made and then measuring actual program performance on the basis of these criteria. The problem with much of what still passes as "evaluation" in local government is that it deals solely with the "front end" of service delivery—inputs such as expenditure amounts, staff size and qualifications, or the facilities and materials available—or focuses on the service-delivery *process* itself, including such characteristics as types and extent of various activities conducted, techniques used, and workload measures.[5] While these are certainly important aspects of program design and operation, examination of these factors alone cannot provide an indication of overall program performance. True performance evaluation, however, should center on the end products of the program, its results or what it really accomplishes.

The type of evaluation of concern in this book focuses attention on program *effectiveness*, determining the extent to which a program is achieving or failing to achieve its stated objectives. Effectiveness measures are indicators of the real, substantive change or improvement produced by a program, the extent to which the desired results of the program are in fact occurring. Concentrating the emphasis of a program evaluation on effectiveness measures, then, gears the whole undertaking to outcomes-oriented criteria rather than more limited process- or operations-oriented criteria.

A second type of performance criterion, which is employed less frequently in the cases presented in this book, is *efficiency*. Efficiency measures serve to get a reading on the extent to which wasted efforts are being minimized or the degree to which the program is maximizing the production of positive results per unit of input. These include *cost-effectiveness* measures which generally compare the direct dollar costs of operating the program to the products which result, as well as indicators of *internal operating efficiency* which represent input/output type relationships at earlier stages of the service-delivery process. In either case, efficiency measures should be subordinated to effectiveness criteria; if a program approach is not capable of producing the desired kinds of results, then the efficiency level at which it is operating is immaterial. However, if the program is producing the kind of substantive change that is intended, then increasing its efficiency may also lead to increased effectiveness. The case studies illustrated here include the use of efficiency measures in instances where the program was aimed in part at improving efficiency, such as increasing the percentage of transit system operating costs which are recovered through the farebox. In other instances, the cases could easily be expanded to incorporate various other types of efficiency measures as subordinated to the effectiveness indicators which serve as the primary basis of evaluation.

Furthermore, the evaluation approach presented here is not geared to assessing performance in light of the larger issues of *appropriateness, economic efficiency,* or *equity*—whether the program's objectives are worthwhile in the first place, whether the total benefits resulting from the program outweight the total costs incurred by it, and whether the distribution of these costs and benefits is fair to all parties concerned. These questions are the subject of more macro-level policy analysis, but it should be kept in mind that measures or estimates of program effectiveness would necessarily feed into these broader kinds of analysis.

The evaluation approach taken in this book, then, stresses the importance of determining the extent to which a program is satisfying its objectives and sometimes incorporates efficiency measures as secondary criteria. Measuring effectiveness requires the evaluator to look beyond program operations to examine whether the program has produced its intended effects or impacts, the extent to which it has improved the conditions, alleviated the problems, or met the needs out in the *environment* which it was designed to deal with in the first place. The basic assumption is that if a program is not producing positive changes, or benefits, in the environment, it does not justify the expenditure of scarce public resources. Thus, ways should be sought to increase the effectiveness of a poorly performing program, or it should be scrapped in favor of some more promising approach. Effectiveness criteria should be prime considerations in the minds of those who are planning or managing public programs, particularly new or innovative programs. Often, however, such people do not have a clear idea of what the actual effectiveness level of a given program is or which of a few alternative program approaches is likely to be most favorable. Thus the purpose of an effectiveness-oriented evaluation, as opposed to a "seat of the pants" or "conventional wisdom" approach to assessing program performance, is to employ a legitimate research approach to ascertain whether a program is meeting its objectives.

Formative Evaluation

Another aspect of the kind of evaluation discussed in this book is its *formative* nature.[6] It is intended to provide input into a continuing planning and programming process in which programs might be modified or even dramatically altered on the basis of evaluation results. *Summative* evaluations, by contrast, are after-the-fact assessments of whether the program did or did not work. The point here is that formative evaluations should be keyed to making recommendations for program improvement, where warranted, based on an understanding of the reasons or explanations for observed results. For the most part, this entails an analysis of the ongoing operation of the program along with the salient environmental factors to find out why the program is or is not performing as expected. This linking of program *process* with *performance* is aimed at developing an understanding of the "whys and wherefores" of success or failure as a basis of suggesting ways for improving performance. Thus, while "front end" input and process variables are not really appropriate evaluative criteria in their own right, incorporating them in the analysis as relevant explanatory factors can be valuable in terms of understanding a program's performance and finding ways to improve its effectiveness.

Formative evaluations are most appropriate for providing feedback on the performance of new programs or those which are being implemented on a trial or demonstration basis. When there is little to go on in terms of past experience with a particular program approach, it is often more important to learn about its strengths and weaknesses, those aspects which seem to be working better than others, and the relationships among factors which both facilitate and inhibit success, rather than to obtain a single summary indication of its end result. Even with a "continue-discontinue" type of decision pending, such an approach can provide valuable insight as to the potential of a program that has not been very successful to date, along with indications of how its performance can be improved if it is to be continued or expanded. More typical, however, is the developmental process through which new program approaches are initiated, tested, modified, and then implemented in alternative versions in the search for a validated approach which should be implemented on a full-scale basis.

Aside from new, innovative programs, the formative-evaluation approach is particularly suited for use with more traditional ongoing programs when it is clear to management that program performance is poor or deteriorating, but the reasons for this or ways in which the situation could be reversed are not readily apparent. The cases discussed in this book involve both new and more traditional programs. In either case, the findings of such evaluations often show that programs are not performing very effectively or at best produce mixed results. In such circumstances, one of the most valuable contributions an evaluation can make is to explain the reasons behind program failure. Clear identification of the weak points in the program's design or the aspects of a program which were implemented poorly is the first and often most important step in developing sound recommendations for improved program management.

Along these lines the evaluations presented in this book utilize the *systems approach* to facilitate identification of the linkages connecting program design features and intended effects, as well as salient environmental factors which should be included in the analysis.[7] The evaluation approach discussed in this book uses systems analysis to develop a substantive framework for the analysis, identifying the relevant variables and the assumed relationships among them. The systems approach is used to structure the problem by picturing the logic of cause-effect sequences on which the program design is based. It is particularly useful for the type of evaluation of interest here because it organizes the variables in a way which is keyed to the attainment of program objectives; specifying the program as a system represents the program as a conversion process in which resources are consumed and activities are conducted in order to produce the desired results. The systems perspective, then, takes inputs and process measures into account as they relate to program effectiveness.

Quasi-Experimental Designs

In terms of research methodology, the case studies incorporate aspects of nonexperimental and particularly quasi-experimental designs based on comparisons that are more readily available than those which might be developed in more highly structured formalized experiments.[8] Measuring program effectiveness requires that the evaluator be able to distinguish between real program effects and those resulting in similar situations in which no program was operating. Quasi-experimental designs are advantageous precisely because they do provide for program/no-program type comparisons which, if appropriately suited to the particular program and its environment, can lead to valid conclusions about program performance. Although the research designs discussed in this book certainly lack the full scientific rigor of true experiments, in which cases are randomly assigned to treatments, quasi-experimental designs can often be used with confidence if care is taken in fitting the design to the particular problem and its context.

For local project evaluations, such lower-level designs are often appropriate, and they are usually less costly and more easy to implement than more structured, true experimental designs.[9] A major characteristic of the evaluation approach being presented here is its relatively low cost; the cases reported here rely on available secondary data and routinely collected program-operation data as much as possible. In fact, a principal strategy utilized here for providing information feedback on program performance is simply to organize and make better use of data which are already existing but largely ignored.

Perhaps more important, quasi-experimental designs generally require much less interference with program implementation and management than do the more sophisticated experimental designs. While weaknesses in the evaluation strategy or in the interpretation of research findings often arise as a result of the way in which a program was implemented or failed to be implemented, for the most part local program evaluation designs can be tailored to fit conditions dictated by the program design and the way it is being carried out. This, of course, makes evaluation more feasible than would be the case if the program design and implementation plans had to be reconfigured in order to permit a sound evaluation.

Case Studies

The similarities and differences among the three programs discussed in this book make them an interesting set of case illustrations. All three—the Harrisburg Housing-Rehabilitation Program, the Williamsport Transit-Improvement Program, and the York Crime-Prevention Program—are basically federally funded programs which are planned, implemented, and administered by city hall. The Harrisburg Housing-Rehabilitation Program, however, is part of a larger ongoing community development program utilizing funds from the Department of Housing and Urban Development (HUD), while the York Crime-Prevention Program (focusing mainly on burglaries) is funded from money made available to the Governor's Justice Commission in Pennsylvania by the Law Enforcement Assistance Administration (LEAA). The evaluations of both these programs were planned as the programs themselves were being initiated.

The Williamsport Transit-Improvement Program differs from the other two in that it concerns a basic service which had already been provided as a public service by the city for quite a few years and before that had been operated by private enterprise. As a city service, the bus system has been generously subsidized by the federal and state departments of transportation (DOT and PennDOT, respectively). The "program" that is being evaluated here is indeed an improvement program rather than a distinctly new program. Thus, while the Harrisburg Housing-Rehabilitation Program and the York Crime-Prevention Program were being implemented on a somewhat restricted basis and evaluated for the first time, the Williamsport Transit-Improvement Program was really the product of an evaluation–plan–modification–reevaluation exercise applied to an already existing full-fledged public service.

All three programs represent local governmental responses to priority problems. General purpose community surveys conducted in Harrisburg and York showed that preventing crime and improving housing conditions are viewed by citizens in both cities as the two top priority problems facing city government.[10] From the local perspective, at least, both these programs were considered as innovative approaches, promising program strategies that were being initiated as new attempts to deal with long-standing entrenched problems that were of deep concern to the citizenry. Improving the performance of the city-owned bus system in Williamsport, on the other hand, was accorded a high priority by a new mayor and his administration, who inherited an operation that had experienced deteriorating service levels and rapid escalations in costs along with drastic decreases in ridership in the preceding two years. The new managers therefore were determined to find out the root causes of these problems and discover ways of improving overall performance. In all three cases there was clearly a lack of certainty as to whether these program strategies or improvements could, in fact, produce the desired results.

Evaluation Approaches

While the same overall evaluation approach was applied in each of the case studies, there is of necessity considerable variation in the specifics of their research designs. The housing-rehabilitation and crime-prevention cases utilize somewhat similar evaluations in that both programs are targeted on neighborhoods or city blocks; they are oriented to geographic areas rather than to individual client characteristics such as a drug-abuse program might be. Therefore, in both these evaluations the household, the city block, the neighborhood, or even the census tract might be appropriate units of analysis. The Harrisburg Housing-Rehabilitation Program, however, is more directly targeted—being implemented for the first phase in two very specifically delineated districts in the city—while the York Crime-Prevention

Program turned out to be implemented in blocks scattered on a more widespread basis across the city. As will be seen, this difference has implications for the ways in which these programs can be evaluated.

The fact that both these programs were implemented on a city-block or neighborhood basis facilitated the analysis of comparisons among geographic areas to discern program/no program differences. The Williamsport Transit-Improvement Program, by contrast, was developed with respect to the system's entire service area, which includes the whole city as well as portions of several adjoining jurisdictions. Although the analysis of needs and service levels was disaggregated to examine general neighborhoods and bus routes separately as well as in combination, the effects of the transit-improvement program were intended to impact on the whole service area. These circumstances did not permit the use of program/no-program comparisons on an area basis, and therefore an alternative evaluation format was required.

With respect to the research designs themselves, the York Crime-Prevention Program and the Williamsport Transit-Improvement Program evaluations employed different variations of time-series analysis, taking a longitudinal approach to compare trends which were developing before the programs were put into effect with the results which materialized afterwards. The plan-modification portion of the transit-improvement case also involved considerable descriptive examination of how the system was currently operating. The housing-rehabilitation evaluation is based on a combination of research design features, a "patched up" design in a sense, but basically it relies on simple before and after comparisons and comparisons between the two program target areas and a no program area. In addition, the housing-rehabilitation evaluation in some respects relies on a simple case-study approach.

The cases also vary in terms of the data bases employed. The housing-rehabilitation evaluation is an example of the usefulness of routine program operation data for monitoring and evaluation purposes, as complemented by the use of external measures of effectiveness. To an even greater degree, the transit-system evaluation entailed a considerable amount of formatting, processing, and making intelligent use of information which for the most part had always been available but had not been maintained in a fashion that lent itself to analysis. The transit study also differs from the other two cases in that it utilizes a wide variety of performance measures drawn from different data sources.

The crime-prevention program evaluation, on the other hand, for the most part relies on police department records which are maintained independently of any specific programs but which were nevertheless organized on a format compatible with the needs of that particular evaluation. In addition, unlike the other two cases, the crime-prevention evaluation depends basically on a single indicator or set of indicators as measures of effectiveness, but it also employs very specific indicators of the process side of the program's implementation. Finally, while all three evaluations do involve the use of primary data, particularly survey interview data, the housing and transit-system evaluations required much more varied and time-consuming data-collection procedures. Consequently, while all three evaluations are considered to be relatively low-cost efforts, the crime-prevention evaluation was substantially less expensive and time-consuming than the other two illustrations.

Outline of the Book

The organization of this book is intended to present an overview of a suggested approach to program evaluation in smaller cities, illustrate it with case studies, and then discuss several issues pertaining to both the design and conduct of evaluations in general. The next two chapters present the approach, discussing the main considerations to be thought through in designing a formative evaluation of program effectiveness. Chapter 2 sets out the systems approach for structuring the problem and discusses various types of effectiveness indicators and data sources, while chapter 3 considers some alternative research designs which might be applicable depending on the operating context and available data.

Chapters 4 through 9 contain the case studies, evaluations of the Harrisburg Housing-Rehabilitation Program, the Williamsport Transit-Improvement Program, and the York Crime-Prevention Program in that order. Each case is presented first in one chapter in terms of the design and implementation of the program itself along with the particular evaluation design to be employed, followed by a chapter which discusses the findings and implications of the actual evaluation. The book concludes with discussions of methodological problems and practical issues regarding the design and conduct of local program evaluation, generalizing from the experiences of the three preceding case studies. Chapter 10 points out problems in research approach and suggests ways in which such evaluations can be strengthened, while chapter 11 discusses their feasibility, costs, and utility for local government.

Notes

1. Edward A. Suchman, *Evaluative Research: Principles and Practice in Public Service and Social Action Programs* (New York: Sage, 1967); Carol H. Weiss (ed.), *Evaluating Action Programs: Readings in Social Ac-*

tion and Education (Boston: Allyn and Bacon, 1972); Harry P. Hatry, Richard E. Winnie, and Donald M. Fisk, *Practical Program Evaluation for State and Local Government Officials* (Washington: Urban Institute, 1973); Jack L. Franklin and Jean H. Thrasher, *An Introduction to Program Evaluation* (New York: Wiley, 1976); and Lynn Morris and Carol Fitzgibbons, *Evaluator's Handbook* (Beverly Hills, Calif.: Sage, 1978), are representative of the writing in this field.

2. Hatry, Winnie, and Fisk, *Practical Program Evaluation.*

3. Rackham S. Fukuhara, "Productivity Improvement in Cities," *The Municipal Yearbook 1977* (Washington: International City Management Association, 1977), p. 196.

4. See Theodore H. Poister, *Public Program Analysis: Applied Research Methods* (Baltimore: University Park Press, 1978), for a comprehensive text on program evaluation.

5. Hatry, Winnie, and Fisk, *Practical Program Evaluation*, pp. 13-15.

6. Michael Scriven, "The Methodology of Evaluation," in Weiss (ed.), *Evaluating Action Programs: Readings in Social Action and Education.* Also, see Carol H. Weiss, *Evaluation Research* (Englewood Cliffs, N.J.: Prentice-Hall, 1972), pp. 16-17.

7. C.W. Churchman, *The Systems Approach* (New York: Delta, 1968); Poister, *Public Program Analysis: Applied Research Methods*, chap. 2.

8. Donald T. Campbell and Julian C. Stanley, *Experimental and Quasi-Experimental Designs for Research* (New York: Rand McNally, 1963).

9. Public Technology, Inc., *Program Evaluation and Analysis: A Technical Guide for State and Local Governments* (Washington: 1978).

10. Theodore H. Poister and James C. McDavid, *A Report of York Residents' Evaluations and Preferences for Local Governmental Programs and Services* (University Park: Institute of Public Administration, Pennsylvania State University, 1977); and Theodore H. Poister, James C. McDavid and Susan K. Miller, *A Report of Harrisburg Residents' Evaluations and Preferences for Local Governmental Programs and Services* (University Park: Institute of Public Administration, Pennsylvania State University, 1976).

2 Structuring the Problem

Introduction

Moving through the design and conduct of a program evaluation requires that the evaluator become thoroughly familiar with the substantive design and intent of the program, develop measures which will indicate whether the program is operating as intended and achieving its stated objectives, and collect and analyze real-world data to address these questions. While there is obviously overlap and some two-directional feedback among these tasks, rather than a strict sequencing, the evaluation approach taken in this book proceeds through the following seven steps:

1. *Identification of objectives and specification of program design.* Any formative evaluation of effectiveness requires a clear understanding of the objectives which the program is intended to accomplish and the underlying logic of program design—how the operating program is expected to attain these objectives.

2. *Development of evaluative criteria and statement of research questions.* This involves developing specific substantive criteria, based on the objectives just identified, on which to assess program effectiveness. The principal research questions concern whether these performance criteria have been or are being met, while secondary or supporting research questions relate to intermediate milestones in the program's operation.

3. *Development of measures and identification of data sources.* In practice this step is often bound up in the issue of research design (discussed next), but in theory it should precede it. Given the evaluative criteria and research questions just identified, the problem facing the evaluator is to develop valid *operationalized indicators* which do measure the extent to which the criteria are being satisfied and represent the other factors contained in the research questions. In deciding what measures to use, consideration also must be given to the sources of the data, their availability, and the cost of collecting the desired information.

4. *Design of the overall research approach.* Developing the *research design* is in many respects the most crucial aspect of a program evaluation. This step concerns determining what observations will be made at what point(s) in time and basically hinges on the issue of what comparisons will be made in order to test whether the program is producing its desired effects. As will be seen, this search for "fair comparisons" may be greatly

facilitated if the evaluation is built into the plan for implementing the program in the first place.

5. *Data collection and processing.* This is often the most expensive and time-consuming part of the evaluation. While data collection often seems like a fairly mechanical process, in other respects it may be highly sensitive to distortions that can invalidate a study's findings. One issue that arises frequently in this regard is the extent to which routine program operation data, which may accumulate on a day-to-day basis, are recorded accurately and completely and can serve as evaluative information.

6. *Data analysis and interpretation.* Conclusions about program performance are drawn from interpretations about what the data show, based on an examination of individual "outcomes" variables and, particularly in a formative evaluation, patterns of associations among numerous variables. The statistical analysis may be quite simple and descriptive only, or it may be more sophisticated, introducing multiple "control" variables or making statistical inferences based on sample data, but in any case the ability to draw firm conclusions depends more on the strength of the overall research design than on the ensuing statistical analysis.

7. *Report writing and dissemination.* Since the purpose of program analysis is to make a positive contribution to planning, programming, and program decision making in general, high-quality evaluation research is not worth anything if it is not aimed at utilization. This requires that findings, conclusions, and recommendations be communicated clearly to those who are in positions to utilize the results.

The first four of the preceding tasks concern the *design* of an evaluation, while the last three involve its *conduct*, the implementation of an evaluation project as developed in steps one through four. The design phase can be summarized as a series of questions to be addressed by the evaluator:

1. What effect is the program supposed to produce, and how is it intended to do this?
2. What specific criteria are appropriate for evaluating program performance, and what substantive issues should be addressed by the evaluation effort?
3. How can we measure the effects and other factors incorporated in the research questions, and what are the sources of these data?
4. What observations can be made, and what comparisons can be structured in order to provide a fair test of whether the program is actually producing its intended effects?

This chapter discusses an approach to the first two tasks, developing a *substantive framework* for the evaluation by identifying objectives, describing the program design, and establishing relevant criteria for measuring performance.

Objectives and Program Design

Structuring the problems to be analyzed in a program evaluation requires a thorough familiarity with the program's objectives, operating design, and environment. For an effectiveness evaluation to be valid, the research questions and hypotheses which are tested should relate to the attainment of worthwhile objectives and the operation of the program as it facilitates or impedes their accomplishment. Thus the first problem in a program evaluation—asking the right questions or focusing on the right problems—depends on an understanding of the program's objectives and the design of the program as it is intended to lead to their accomplishment, along with the environmental factors which might influence a program's success or failure.

Any structured program design is based on an underlying logic which consists of presumed cause-and-effect relationships. In essence, the *program logic* explains how the use of resources in varied program activities is expected to produce tangible effects that represent the attainment of objectives. A description of this logic can be thought of as a series of "if, then" type statements which, taken in sequence, represent a chain of cause-effect linkages that are expected to lead from the initial use of resources to the production of desired impacts. Depending on a program's nature and scope, the set of linkages may be simple or complex. A simple two-step description of the logic underlying a building-codes enforcement program, for example, might be: (1) inspecting dwelling units will product citations for those which are out of compliance with codes, and (2) citing substandard dwelling units for noncompliance will induce property owners to bring them into compliance. Lining out these assumptions will help first of all to clarify what the program is supposed to be doing, and second, it will provide a way of backtracking to identify points at which the program logic or implementation might break down. For example, if the codes-enforcement program just mentioned is found not to lead to a decrease in the number of substandard dwelling units, is it because substandard units were not cited or because the citations failed to have the predicted effect on property owners' actions?

Identification of Objectives

Program objectives concern production of physical, socioeconomic, behavioral, or psychological changes which are beneficial to participants, target populations, or the society as a whole. These changes are the program's effects on the environment and should be the justification of the program in the first place. In the process of planning for new or substantially revised public programs, the objectives should be established first and the design oriented toward achieving them. In practice, program staff, program managers, and even program planners often lose sight of exactly what the objectives are; moreover, a clear definition of the underlying program logic may be impossible. Thus, identifying the objectives a program is supposedly keyed to and defining the underlying program logic often involves a process of reconstructing the overall design of a program that may well be operating on a day-to-day basis with only a vague idea about what its objectives really are.

Program objectives should be clearcut statements of specific and measurable expected results. To the degree possible, they should be specified not only in terms of the type of effects anticipated, but also as to the expected magnitude of effects and the time frame within which they can reasonably be expected to materialize. From both a management and an evaluative perspective, specifying objectives in these terms should be done realistically; objectives should be thought of as concrete milestones which the program should be able to produce. In the context of one of the programs considered in this book, for example, evaluating a crime-prevention program in light of whether or not burglaries were completely eliminated would be totally unrealistic. The objective as set forth in the York Crime-Prevention Program—to reduce the incidence of burglaries by 5.0 percent in one year—would, on the other hand, appear to present a fair basis of evaluation. Clearly, specifying objectives to this extent is a judgmental process. While objectives should not be so overly ambitious as to be out of reach for all practical purposes, if they are too modest, the result may well be an automatic positive evaluation of a program with little practical significance.

A second consideration in delineating the objectives of a program is that often there are various levels of objectives which may be linked together as an elaboration of the underlying program logic. For example, the immediate effects of the program also may be expected to contribute to intermediate or subsequent effects, which might be further expected to trigger additional, longer-range impacts. As an illustration, one immediate objective of the Harrisburg Housing-Rehabilitation Program is to eliminate abandoned houses and other buildings that constitute hazards to public safety. If this does in fact occur, then the program will have produced an immediate effect which is worthwhile in its own right. However, this effect is also intended to contribute to improved attitudes of residents toward their neighborhoods, which in turn might be expected to produce the subsequent impact of reducing the outmigration of residents from the neighborhoods to other parts of the city.

Frequently, evaluators encounter situations in which program managers and staff personnel do not seem to have a clear idea of what the program's objectives are, or they may have conflicting views as to what the objectives should be. In dealing with new programs, planners may be almost totally concerned with the gearing up and initial implementation processes at the expense of thinking in more forward-looking terms about real substantive objectives. With ongoing, more traditional programs, officials often drift into a state of great concern with routine activities and internal operating efficiency while losing sight of what the program should be all about. Furthermore, most programs are characterized by multiple objectives, and especially when these have evolved over time in a casual way, some may even be contradictory to others.

In the absence of clearcut objectives around which there is a strong consensus, a number of strategies are available to the analyst. First, he can attempt to force the objectives from program personnel, and this might well be a healthy exercise for them, if it can be made to work. Second, he can define the objectives himself based on observation and familiarity with the program, previous studies done on similar programs, written guidelines and regulations that may apply, and points of view solicited from any interested parties. In order to avoid too narrow a focus based on the analyst's own values, the safest approach here is to try to maintain a balance by including all the objectives that surface in the review, regardless of incompatibilities. Third, the evaluation can start with an open-ended approach, beginning with a number of broad goal statements and working with program personnel in successive rounds of attempts to refine them into a set of specific objectives. This last approach may be the wisest,[1] particularly in emerging program areas where in general there is little consensus as to what constitutes success.

Situations where the program analyst is, in fact, directly involved in operating the program offer some special advantages and disadvantages. The main advantage such a person has is a familiarity with program operations that permits a more realistic specification of objectives and a more accurate detailing of program design; often it is also less time consuming. The main advantage also stems from the analyst's closeness to the program. Objectivity, keeping expectations and preferences for outcomes to a minimum, is difficult. Program administrators are often evaluated by their superiors on the basis of how "successful" a program appears to be. The temptation is to introduce biases that make the program look good. Administrative rationality might make such a strategy personally worthwhile, but there may also be a loss of important information which could be used to make sound modifications to a program.

Unanticipated Impacts

The importance of realistically identifying a program's objectives stems from the fact that effectiveness evaluations are concerned with determining whether the intended impacts—which are derived from the objectives—are in fact being produced. A full-fledged evaluation, particularly a formative evaluation, should also encompass impacts which are not intentional and which may not be desirable. Unanticipated impacts are even more difficult to identify because they may not be suggested by the program logic. In some cases programs have almost the opposite effects from those which are intended and exacerbate the problems they are aimed at alleviating. In a housing program, for example, a rigid codes-enforcement component might have the adverse effect of encouraging the abandonment of marginal properties, leading to a decrease in the available housing stock and further neighborhood deterioration.

Weiss makes the point that unanticipated effects can be negative, neutral, or even good, as in a reading-skills educational program which, in addition to improved reading ability, might lead to improved conduct at home as well as at school.[2] Furthermore, with some programs there may be potential negative impacts which are certainly not intentional but which can be anticipated. A halfway house program which serves both hardened criminals and first offenders may have to mix these clientele groups as a result of financial necessity, although it may be anticipated that this contact will have some adverse effect on some of the first offenders. Thus a thorough effectiveness evaluation should look at all four possible categories of impacts, as represented in table 2-1.

The identification of unanticipated impacts is one of the most challenging aspects of program analysis and planning and one of the reasons why analysts and evaluators need to be familiar with the substantive aspects of a program as well as with research tools. Weiss recommends that evaluators brainstorm about all the possible unanticipated effects of a program in advance of structuring projects, while remaining flexible enough to incorporate those which emerge later in their analysis.[3]

Systems Analysis

The approach to specifying the logic of program design advocated in this book is *systems analysis*, which for our purposes can be defined as the analysis of a program as a set of interacting elements aimed at achieving some common overall objective(s).[4] Most programs do consist of multiple *components* or subsystems, and these components might be broken down into further subsystems or *elements*. A key feature of the systems approach is the identification of relationships among the components as they affect the attainment of overall program objectives. Used either in developing a program in the first place or in reconstructing its underlying logic later on for purposes of evaluation, the systems approach is a useful organizing tool

Table 2-1
Categories of Potential Program Impact

	Anticipated	Unanticipated
Positive	a	b
Negative	b	b

[a]Derived from program objectives.
[b]Side effects or byproducts.

because (1) it treats program activities as integral parts of larger entities rather than in isolation, and (2) it ties these activities to specific objectives. Inherent in this approach is an attempt to avoid suboptimization by linking short-run immediate subsystem objectives to longer-range subsequent program impacts.

As presented in this book, systems analysis is really an organizing tool for building a substantive framework for the evaluation, determining what variables should be included in the analysis and what issues they will be used to examine. In addition to identifying objectives, this entails becoming familiar with the substance of the program and its context and learning how the program is (or was) intended to function, particularly how various components are expected to interact and contribute to attainment of the program's overall objectives. The product of this exercise in "systematic thinking" should be a model of the program design which identifies the critical variables and the presumed relationships among them. These variables include environmental factors, program or process measures, linking variables, and effectiveness measures, as shown in figure 2-1.

Clearly, the extent to which the type of model represented in figure 2-1 is elaborated will depend on the complexity of the program as well as the amount of effort and detail being contemplated for the evaluation. In any case, the analyst should consider the possible relevance of each of these different classes of variables to the evaluation at hand and be aware of the kind of role played by each.

Environmental Variables

A principal feature of systems analysis is the important distinction between those factors which are under control of program management and those which are beyond its control. Many factors which influence program performance are external to the program itself and must be taken as "givens" that cannot be manipulated by program management. *Environmental variables* characterize the operating context of the program. They can be of

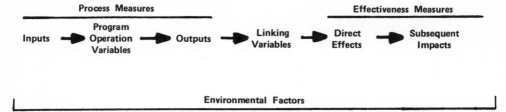

Figure 2-1. Problem-Specification Variables.

a physical, socioeconomic, attitudinal, legal, financial, or institutional nature, and they can act either as constraints or opportunities, factors which inhibit or facilitate a program's success.

A given program strategy may work well in one type of environment but very poorly under other conditions because of differences in these constraints and opportunities. In formative evaluations intended to explain the reasons why programs succeed or fail, then, it is important to identify the relevant environmental variables and incorporate them in the analysis. This contingency of program success on specific environmental characteristics also has implications for the development of research designs, discussed in the following chapter. Basically, if program/no-program comparisons are to be valid, the evaluator will have to "hold constant" the major environmental influences or else find a way to adjust for differences in these effects.

One important dimension of the environment concerns the problems, conditions, or general set of circumstances which give rise to the need for the program in the first place. These factors are sometimes incorporated in the analysis with *need* or *demand indicators*, variables which measure the magnitude of a problem or represent variation in the characteristics of such problems or conditions from case to case. While the general field of needs assessment is a separate aspect of policy analysis in its own right,[5] the inclusion of needs and demand indicators in a program evaluation may be useful in two ways: (1) variation in needs may be helpful in explaining the results of the performance evaluation, and (2) in some instances these indicators can serve as benchmarks against which to measure the program's progress.

Process Measures

The program or process measures as shown in figure 2-1 really describe the program design and the way it is intended to operate. While the resources, or costs, are inputs going into the program, incorporating program operation variables and output measures in the analysis takes us inside the "black box'' of the program's internal operation and facilitates the formative evaluation of program effectiveness.

Resources are the things—usually manpower, money, materials, equipment, and facilities—which are available for use in a program. The activities by which resources (staff time, for instance) are converted into outputs (completed housing inspections, for example) for the most part form the components of the program. While there are constraints on the resources available to any program, the way in which resources are used and the rate at which they are used by various subsystems is largely a matter of managerial control.

Traditionally, many program evaluations have been keyed to an assessment of the quality and quantity of inputs, such as levels of funding and staff qualifications, rather than to real performance evaluation. This is largely because inputs are generally the easiest data to obtain, but such evaluations do not test whether the program actually works. In the type of evaluation discussed in this book, however, resources and program components definitely are taken into account, not as criteria, but rather as independent variables which are expected to have a strong influence on how well a program performs.

While initial resource levels are sometimes analyzed in their own right, program process can be linked to effectiveness measures through the use of *program operation variables*. The degree to which these program operation variables are elaborated depends on both the complexity of the program itself and the type of research design being used. In the most simple case the program might be represented as a single "program/no-program" dichotomy, with some neighborhood blocks being exposed to a burglary-prevention effort and others being outside the target area, for example.

Alternatively, the program operation variables may be further refined, such as the length of time a program has been operating in a certain target area, the amount of information provided in advance of the actual initiation of the program, the particular sequencing of activities and procedures that make up the program, and the particular mix of services which are made available through the program. In general, the more variation there is in terms of how a program is implemented, the more that can be learned about which features or combination of features lead to success. The most useful formative evaluations often concern programs in which alternative strategies are employed side by side for comparative purposes—for instance, a codes-inspection–housing-rehabilitation combined strategy used in one neighborhood as compared with a codes-inspection only strategy used in a separate but similar neighborhood.

However simple or complex the program design, the most direct products of the components are *outputs*, which can be thought of as units of programmed activity. Outputs have no inherent value in and of themselves, but they are an important link in the underlying program logic, which holds that the production of outputs will trigger the occurrence of the desired effects or impacts in the environment. Outputs tend to be measures of workload or work completed, such as the number of codes inspections performed or the number of violations identified. In evaluations of program effectiveness, we are concerned with outputs in two respects: (1) are outputs being produced as planned, and more important, (2) are these outputs leading to the desired impacts?

As mentioned earlier, most programs consist of multiple components and elements, and it is usually informative to examine these separately as well as in terms of interactions among these. Program operation variables are measures which describe these components and elements, and individual components or elements will usually utilize different resources and produce different outputs. Thus in developing a systems framework for a particular program along the lines suggested by figure 2-1, the analyst may well depict separate components with parallel streams of elements and outputs, using arrows to represent intended interrelationships.

Effectiveness Measures

Program effectiveness is measured in terms of meeting objectives. In measuring program effectiveness, we are concerned with whether immediate objectives are being accomplished and, if so, whether they are leading to the attainment of intermediate and ultimate objectives. In this book, the term *direct effects* refers to variables which represent the attainment of the immediate objectives of program components, while the term *impacts* refers to the subsequent, usually broader and often longer-range effects or changes in the environment which are expected to result from the achievement of the program's immediate objectives. Thus the direct effects of a housing-rehabilitation program might be (1) the elimination of abandoned buildings which are nuisances or safety hazards, (2) a reduction in the migration of residents out of an area, (3) an increase in home ownership, and (4) a spinoff of similar benefits to surrounding neighborhoods. Typically, effectiveness measures, especially measures of subsequent impact, are the most difficult to develop good indicators for—certainly they are the most important. The next chapter contains a discussion of various types of alternative or complementary effectiveness measures.

Again depending on the complexity of the program logic, it may be desirable to specify *linking variables*. These represent intermediate results which are expected to connect outputs to direct effects. For example, certain outputs (such as neighborhood meetings conducted) might be aimed at getting residents interested in a program, an intermediate result which is necesssary if the program is to get off the ground and produce direct effects. Linking variables often concern obtaining an initial response to a new program—participation in or utilization of services—while other linking variables represent changes in client characteristics which prompt or permit the real intended effects to occur.

Program Specification

Building this substantive framework is a matter of identifying these different types of variables for the different program components and laying them out in a way that shows their intended relationships. Figure 2-2 is an illustration of this approach applied to an alcoholism recovery center. Its two components are diagnosis and outpatient treatment, each of which is further broken down into elements. Resources are not shown in the figure, but such indicators as staff time or dollar costs could easily be attached to the elements. The element labels themselves actually represent the type of program operation involved, and within each element there really is little variation in service delivery.

The outputs in this case concern the numbers of clients who are screened, referred, treated, etc. These activities have no inherent value in their own right, but are worthwhile only if they result in real benefits. An interesting feature of this particular illustration is that one component, diagnosis, is for the most part a support subsystem rather than one that provides direct service. Its effectiveness would be measured by the extent to which it diagnoses clients correctly and results in their receiving, from some other source, the services that are appropriate for their individual problems. An important point to note along these lines is that a major output of the diagnosis component is the referral of certain clients to the outpatient-treatment component of the same agency's program.

The diagram of the outpatient-treatment component indicates how group therapy, individual therapy, and family therapy/counseling are intended to lead to the client's recovery. Specifically, some intermediate changes must occur, such as increased client awareness of the problem, client recognition that recovery is possible, and increased family understanding and support, as represented by linking variables. Finally, the model indicates that while the intended direct effect is recovery from alcohol-related problems, the subsequent impact which is hoped for is the resocialization of clients into "functional citizens." Obviously, in this program area it will be easier to gain consensus about what "recovery" means than what this "resocialization" implies. Although not included in the diagram, the relevant environmental variables, such as client characteristics, including background and attitude, as well as community characteristics and the availability of other treatment modalities, would have to be incorporated into the analysis.

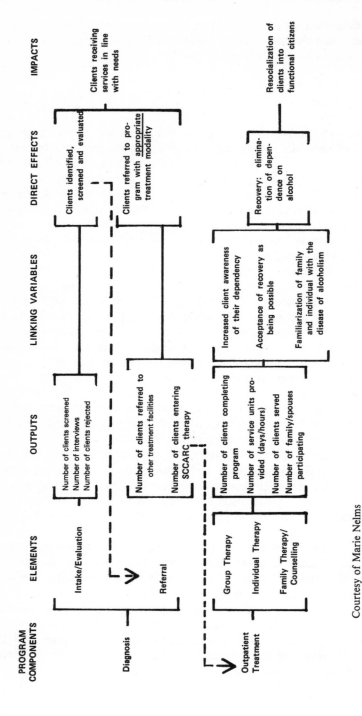

Courtesy of Marie Nelms

Figure 2-2. Systems Model: Southern Chester County Alcoholism Recovery Center (SCCARC).

Process Monitoring

A systems model of a program, such as shown in figure 2-2, facilitates a formative approach by permitting a backtracking through the program logic to examine the process of program operation. In some instances, a convenient way of operationalizing this approach is known as "client tracking." Figure 2-3 shows a charting of the progress of a client through the alcoholism recovery program just described, indicating alternative routes through various elements. Obtaining measures of the number of clients passing through each route during a given period helps to picture the overall

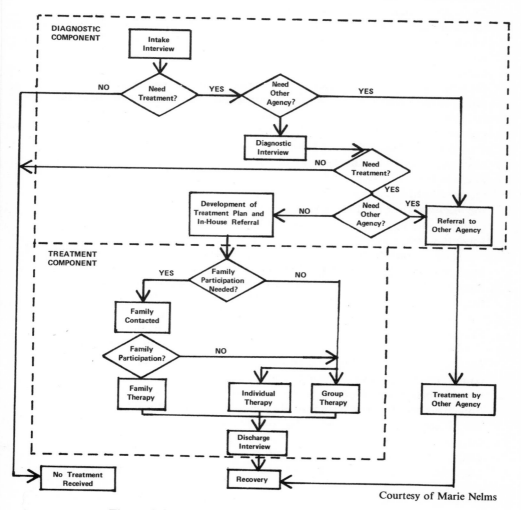

Courtesy of Marie Nelms

Figure 2-3. Client Flow through SCCARC Program.

process of the program. Figure 2-3 is really a flowchart, which is very different from the systems model in figure 2-2. The systems model shows the logic of the assumptions underlying the program design, while the flowchart depicts the sequencing of steps as the program operates on a day-to-day basis.

As shown in figure 2-3, prospective clients contacting the SCCARC for the first time begin with an intake interview. At that point it is determined whether they are indeed in need of treatment and, if so, whether the most appropriate treatment modality is one provided by SCCARC's treatment component or the client should be referred to another treatment agency. Typically, a client who is moving through the SCCARC system then goes on to an indepth diagnostic interview, the result of which is either referral to another agency or, more likely, the development of a treatment plan and in-house referral. The next question is whether family participation is recommended; if so, and the family is willing, the client moves into the family therapy element of SCCARC's outpatient-treatment component. If the family is not needed or is unwilling to participate, the client would move into individual or group therapy. Finally, he would be discharged and presumably would be recovered from his alcohol-related problem. Recovery should also be the end state of those who had been referred to treatment by other agencies, while those who had not been referred to treatment or who had not been willing to undergo treatment would not be expected to have changed their condition. It should be understood that figure 2-3 illustrates the *intended* flow of clients in need of treatment through the SCCARC program; at any point along the way, clients may for whatever reason elect to leave the system before achieving recovery.

As a rational approach to program planning, systems analysis should begin by identifying the desired effects and impacts and work backwards through the sequencing to structure program components and output targets which would appear to be capable of producing these results. This was, in fact, the approach taken in developing both the York Crime-Prevention Program and the Williamsport Transit-Improvement Program.

In ex post facto evaluations in which the program logic is being reconstructed, there may be a tendency to start with inputs and program components and move through to outputs, direct effects, and impacts. This occurs when program personnel are not really certain of what the goals and objectives are. In some instances, they may have a pretty good idea of what the objectives are supposed to be, but not a clear conception of how the ongoing program components are intended to lead to these objectives. This can result in working from both ends toward the middle in order to complete the program logic and often produces a fairly artificial program rationale.

Clearly, these approaches can easily be misused; systems analysis is worthless if it is employed simply to rationalize a program design on paper by linking inputs to outputs to impacts on a series of tenuous assumptions. Yet this same approach can be very useful if taken seriously, that is, *if* the assumptions which make up the program logic do appear reasonable and *if* validity of these assumptions is to be tested by the evaluation.

Performance Criteria and Research Questions

The criteria for evaluating the effectiveness of public programs stem directly from their objectives. Thus they relate to the intended changes or benefits in the environment which the program is expected to produce. Effectiveness criteria should be observable, measurable conditions, and if possible, they should set standards against which actual accomplishments can be measured. When objectives have been clearly specified with respect to magnitude of effects and time frame, such standards are already given. The Williamsport Transit-Improvement Program, for example, was keyed to the objective of increasing ridership by 10 percent within a year.

As indicated earlier, however, statements of objectives are not always this specific. In such instances, evaluators basically have two options: (1) try to determine what level of performance could reasonably be expected and set standards accordingly, or (2) in the absence of specified standards, use open-ended research questions and proceed without clearcut criteria. With this second approach, the practical significance of the program's results will have to be assessed after its effects have been measured. This may still be an appropriate procedure, since the purpose of this type of evaluation is not simply to rate the program as a success or failure, but rather to measure the extent to which it is producing the intended impacts and suggest ways of improving performance.

Research Questions

As indicated earlier, the principal research questions concern the effects on the environment produced by the program. Whether the objectives indicate specific standards or not, the major hypotheses should represent the underlying logic, which holds that the program will exert some *causal influence* in producing the intended benefits. For example, in the York Crime-Prevention Program it is hypothesized that the program *will have produced* a 5 percent decrease in burglaries. In the Harrisburg Housing-Rehabilitation Program, it would be hypothesized that the program is *responsible for* dwelling units being brought into compliance with codes.

The important point to be understood regarding these research questions is that they are *cause-effects-oriented* hypotheses, assumptions about cause-effect relationships upon which the whole program logic is built. This causal nature of the hypotheses is the central concern in the development of an adequate research design, as will become apparent later. Basically, in order for this type of hypothesis to be corroborated, it must be shown that the intended effects did in fact materialize and that the program was responsible for them.

In addressing those hypotheses concerned directly with a program's effects, we are interested in testing the theory or logic underlying the program. Essentially, this logic says that if the program is implemented and operated as planned, the intended benefits will result. In order to test the logic, then, the evaluator must ascertain whether or not the program has in fact been implemented and operated according to its design.

This issue leads to consideration of supporting hypotheses which relate to the program operation itself. These *program-oriented* hypotheses are keyed to measures of output; in general they relate to whether the program is producing outputs as planned, perhaps in terms of both quality and quantity. If observed output indicators do meet the targets established for them, the program can be considered to have been implemented as planned and operating on schedule.

The idea of examining program-oriented hypotheses concerned with outputs in conjunction with effects-oriented hypotheses concerned with impacts is the key to linking effectiveness evaluations to process studies. If output indicators can be linked with measures of effectiveness, this can often lead to increased understanding of how and why a program performs as it does, as well as to suggestions for improvement. An important point here is that in formative evaluations it is essential to know *why* certain programs are ineffective. In general, there are two types of explanations, as shown in figure 2-4: (1) the logic underlying the program does not hold up, or (2) the program was not implemented well in the first place.

In order to test the program's logic, it must be implemented and operating as planned. First, if output targets are not being met, there is a *failure in program* and the logic has not been tested fairly. Thus the next

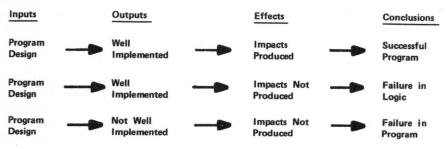

Inputs	Outputs	Effects	Conclusions
Program Design	Well Implemented	Impacts Produced	Successful Program
Program Design	Well Implemented	Impacts Not Produced	Failure in Logic
Program Design	Not Well Implemented	Impacts Not Produced	Failure in Program

Figure 2-4. Types of Program Failure.

step would be to correct the internal operation of the program, get the outputs on target, and then evaluate its effectiveness. Alternatively, a close assessment of the reasons behind the failure in the program might indicate that the program design is not feasible for the given operating environment. This would be a worthwhile finding in its own right. Second, if the analysis indicates that output targets have been met but that the program still has not been effective, there is a *failure in logic*, that is, some part of the underlying logic is invalid. Ideally, a more refined analysis of the intermediate linkages in the underlying logic and/or an analysis of the effects of environmental variables can lead to suggestions for revising the program design with an increased likelihood of achieving effective results.

Notes

1. Carol H. Weiss, *Evaluation Research* (Englewood Cliffs, N.J.: Prentice-Hall, 1972), p. 28.
2. Ibid., p. 33.
3. Ibid.
4. See C. West Churchman, *The Systems Approach* (New York: Delta, 1968) for a general introduction to this perspective. See Theodore H. Poister, *Public Program Analysis: Applied Research Methods* (Baltimore: University Park Press, 1978), chapter 2 for a fuller discussion of the systems approach applied to program evaluation.
5. Wayne A. Kimmel, *Needs Assessment: A Critical Perspective* (Washington: Department of Health, Education and Welfare, 1977).

3 Developing the Research Design

Given a statement of program objectives and the relevant issues to be addressed in an effectiveness evaluation, the next task is to develop a research approach to the problem. This involves consideration of what indicators to use in operationalizing the various types of measures as well as the development of a research design, the basic analytical framework for drawing conclusions about program performance. These two steps must be thought through together, and as will become apparent, they involve the consideration of time, cost, and feasibility issues in addition to concerns about sound research methodology.

Measures and Data Sources

Having identified the relevant program and environmental variables to be examined in an evaluation, one must operationalize them by developing measures or indicators which adequately represent them. Essentially, operationalizing a variable means identifying the source of data and the procedure for taking the measure. For example, we might decide to use the number of building permits as an indicator of the rate of repairs and improvements to properties in certain neighborhoods; the measure would be operationalized by searching through city hall records on building permits and noting all permits for properties in these neighborhoods over the time period of interest.

This development of operationalized indicators is a critical step in the evaluation procedure because it defines the quality of the data on which the evaluation is based. In addition, the selection of measures also depends on considerations of time and effort costs of data collection, and evaluators often are faced with tradeoffs between the quality of the data and the feasibility of collecting it. As will become clear, the usefulness of potential data sources is also dependent in part on the type of research design to be used.

Many different types of data are used in program evaluations, and any given evaluation may well employ data taken from a number of sources. One helpful distinction here is that between *primary data*, which are original data collected firsthand specifically for a given evaluation, and *secondary data*, which are already in existence but lend themselves to the

31

purposes of the evaluation. Secondary data that are commonly used in program evaluations include (1) routine program-operation data which accumulate as part of service-delivery or program-management procedures, (2) records maintained by governmental agencies or other institutions, and (3) regularly published data such as the *U.S. Census of Population*. Relevant types of primary data include (1) interview surveys of program staff, participants, or the community at large, and (2) direct observation methods such as tests or physical inspections.[1]

Reliability and Validity

While in some instances there may be an obvious choice of a measure that is suitable for testing a particular hypothesis, there are other cases in which it is much less clear which, if any, possible indicators should be preferred. This sometimes reflects the paradoxical situation in which a program or agency is seemingly swamped with a proliferation of data with little or no apparent use, while evaluators claim that there is a lack of adequate data for assessing program performance.

Very often the variables which prove most difficult to operationalize, and the most costly, are those intended to measure a program's effectiveness.[2] In general, from a methodological standpoint it is highly desirable to use multiple indicators to measure program effectiveness, but obviously this can make it more difficult to keep reasonable limits on data-collection costs. Examples of alternative or complementary measures of the effectiveness of a city's recreation services suggested by the Urban Institute are shown in table 3-1. Of particular interest here is the mix of citizen-survey data[3] with other types of measures, such as attendance and accident statistics.

The worth of such indicators for use in a given evaluation depends on the degree to which they are *reliable* and *valid* measures of the variables they are used to represent. Briefly, *reliability* refers to the consistency or dependability of a measure over repeated applications, while *validity* refers to the appropriateness of a measure or the extent to which it really represents what it is purported to represent.[4]

Reliability problems are usually thought of in terms of random errors in the data, while systematic errors in the way a measure is taken weaken its validity. Thus reliability is a matter of accuracy and precision, while validity relates to a measure's relevance and whether it might be a biased indicator. For example, if the records on building permits are maintained in a very haphazard way, building-permit data for any given neighborhood in the city may be highly unreliable, undercounted, or overcounted as a matter of chance effect. If, however, the evaluator is concerned that many property owners make large-scale repairs or improvements without securing a per-mit, he is dealing with a problem of validity in that his operationalized in-dicator appears to systematically underestimate the number of properties to which sizable repairs or improvements have been made.

One issue that sometimes arises with respect to valid effectiveness measures is whether the program itself may produce change in the measur-ing instruments. This problem usually involves differential reporting rates that can distort conclusions about program effectiveness. For example, one anticipated effect of the York Crime-Prevention Program was that once the program was implemented in target areas, there would be a greater tendency than before for people to report burglaries to the police. This would have two implications regarding the comparisons to be made: (1) a simple before and after comparison in the target areas could show no decrease in burglary rate, when in fact a real decrease in the number of burglaries was offset by the increased reporting of burglaries, and (2) since no-program comparison areas would not be expected to experience an increase in reporting rates, real differences between the two types of areas could be concealed by their differential rates of reporting burglaries. In this instance, then, victimiza-tion surveys of households to determine actual burglary rates might be preferable to police department statistics, everything else being equal.[5]

Feasibility of Data Collection

The preceding example on measuring burglary rates illustrates the kind of choice that often faces evaluators in selecting indicators of effectiveness. While one type of indicator may be preferable in terms of validity and/or reliability, everything else is *not* always equal. As evidenced in table 3-1, alternative indicators under consideration usually come from different sources and would involve different time and effort costs in data collection. In practice, then, preferred indicators may well require additional costs, and time, money, and other practical considerations may dictate that less satisfactory measures be used instead.

Such choices often boil down to the use of either (1) readily available secondary data, which are more suspect in terms of validity and reliability, or (2) additional primary data, which entail extra cost but are considered superior in terms of reliability and validity. In keeping with the objective of designing low-effort program evaluations which do provide valid results, the position advocated in this book is to use available data whenever pos-sible while still maintaining standards of validity and reliability. Where secondary data do not exist or where the available secondary data are poor, new or additional indicators should be developed. When high-quality in-dicators are simply not feasible, the evaluator can resort to less satisfac-

Table 3-1
Effectiveness Measures for Recreation Services

Overall Objective: To provide for all citizens a variety of enjoyable leisure opportunities that are accessible, safe, physically attractive, and uncrowded.

Objective	Quality Characteristic	Specific Measure	Data-Collection Procedure
Enjoyableness	Citizen satisfaction	1. Percentage of households rating neighborhood park and recreation opportunities as satisfactory.	General citizen survey
	User satisfaction	2. Percentage of those households using community park or recreation facilities who rate them as satisfactory.	General citizen survey or survey of users (of particular facilities)
	Usage–participation	3. Percentage of community households using (or not using) a community park or recreation facility at least once over a specific past period, such as three months. (For nonusers, provide the percentage not using facilities for various reasons, and distinguish reasons that can be at least partly controlled by the government from those which cannot.)	General citizen survey
	Usage–attendance	4. Number of visits at recreation sites.	Attendance statistics and estimates from general citizen survey
Avoidance of crowdedness	User satisfaction	5. Percentage of user households rating crowdedness of community facilities as unsatisfactory.	General citizen survey or survey of users (of particular facilities)
	Nonuser satisfaction	6. Percentage of nonuser households giving crowded conditions as a reason for nonuse of facilities.	General citizen survey

	Characteristic	Measure	Data Source
	Crowding factor	7. Average peak-hour attendance divided by capacity.	Attendance statistics and estimates of carrying capacity
Physical attractiveness	User satisfaction	8. Percentage of user households rating physical attractiveness as satisfactory.	General citizen survey or survey of users (of particular facilities)
	Nonuser satisfaction	9. Percentage of nonuser households rating lack of physical attractiveness as reason for nonuse.	General citizen survey
	Facility cleanliness	10. Percentage of user households rating cleanliness as satisfactory.	General citizen survey or survey of users
	Equipment condition	11. Percentage of user households rating condition of equipment as satisfactory.	General citizen survey or survey of users
Safety	Injuries to participants resulting from accidents	12. Number of serious injuries (for example, those requiring hospitalization) per 10,000 visits.	Accident and attendance statistics
	Criminal incidents	13. Number of criminal incidents per 10,000 visits.	Criminal incident statistics of some park and recreation agencies and most municipal police forces; attendance statistics
	User satisfaction	14. Percentage of user households rating safety of facilities as satisfactory.	General citizen survey or survey of users
	Nonuser satisfaction	15. Percentage of nonuser households giving lack of safety as a reason for nonuse of municipal facilities.	General citizen survey

Source: Hatry et al., *How Effective Are Your Community Services* (Washington: Urban Institute, 1977), p. 42.

tory measures but compensate for anticipated biases in his subjective interpretations.

A final point to be brought out here is that the identification of appropriate measures and data sources should be dealt with in conjunction
with the development of an overall research design, to be discussed in the
following section. There is a two-directional relationship between these two
aspects of program evaluation in that (1) the selection of indicators may
hinge on the type of research design being planned, while (2) the identification of preferred indicators or data constraints may also influence the type
of design which is developed.

The primary point here is that while one desirable feature of a research
design is the comparison of program participants with nonparticipants,
there may be a substantial amount of information on participants that is not
available for nonparticipants. With respect to a housing-rehabilitation program, for example, one major indicator of effectiveness might be the
number of substandard dwelling units brought into code compliance. While
this information is known for the program's target neighborhoods, it may
not be feasible to inspect dwelling units in comparison neighborhoods to
determine their code status. Even when comparable indicators of
postprogram conditions are available, it may be difficult to compare rates
of change because although baseline data are available from preprogram
needs assessments in the target areas, comparable data are not available for
the nonprogram areas. Thus data limitations often constrain the general
type of research design to be employed.

Research Design

The validity of the conclusions arrived at in a program evaluation depends
primarily on the strength of its research design. The design provides the
overall analytical framework within which the evaluation will be conducted;
the definition of operationalized indicators, data-collection procedures, and
statistical analysis are all subordinate to the general approach reflected by
the research design.[6]

An adequate research design is essential for testing the assumptions
about cause-effect relationships which make up the program logic. Basically, the design is a procedure for determining whether the intended impacts actually occur and whether observed effects are the results of program
activity. Without a good design, the evaluator will have greater difficulty in
both determining what changes in impact conditions have occurred and interpreting the causes of his findings.

In order to determine whether a program is producing its intended effects, a research design must be capable of two things: (1) measuring whether

those effects have occurred, and (2) sorting out cause-effect relationships to isolate those effects which can be attributed to the program. This second task is the more challenging one. In its simplest terms, ascertaining whether the program is really responsible for producing observed effects is largely a matter of sorting out the effects of various components of a program or comparing the effects of alternative program strategies. More important, the research design should be capable of differentiating program impacts from the possible effects of trends or shifts in the environment. Furthermore, the design itself should be as free as possible from contaminating influences so that the evaluator can be confident that apparent effects are not pseudo effects of his own methodology, such as a bias in measuring instruments, as discussed in the preceding section.

The classic approach to isolating the effects of public programs would be through experimental design, in which cases are randomly assigned to program and nonprogram groups, treated the same in all respects except whether the program is administered or not, and then monitored and compared in terms of impact measures to determine whether there are significant differences in outcomes between program and nonprogram groups. While such true experiments are far superior from a methodological standpoint, they are rarely used in practice chiefly because they require a degree of control over program implementation and operation which is not considered acceptable, and because in the nonlaboratory real-world context of public programs it would often be very difficult to maintain experimental control over the subjects for the duration of the project.

This book is concerned with lower-level designs which, while less structured and less costly, may be suited for determining whether a program is producing its intended results. These approaches are often called nonexperimental and quasi-experimental designs.[7] Although these lower-level designs lack the scientific rigor of true experiments, they are ''doable'' in small local jurisdictions and they can lead to valid conclusions if applied judiciously.

Noncomparison Designs

In the absence of experimental control and the random assignment of cases to program and nonprogram groups, the major decisions to be made in developing a research design include:

1. Identifying the case or unit of analysis.
2. Identifying which cases or set of cases will be observed.
3. Determining when these observations or measures are to be taken.
4. Establishing which comparisons will be made as the basis for assessing program effectiveness.

Since two of the programs discussed in this book are targeted primarily on neighborhoods, the appropriate unit of analysis could be the census tract, a neighborhood, the city block, or the household. In part the choice depends on what data are available for different units of analysis. With other kinds of programs, each individual program participant might constitute a case. At the other extreme, the program might be citywide in scope, and the unit of analysis or case in question might be the entire city or program. In the Williamsport Transit-Improvement Program evaluation, for example, while much of the planning analysis was based on smaller geographic zones, the evaluation of the improvement program's impact utilized the service area as a whole as the unit of analysis. For example, ridership generated by the entire area was used as a summary measure, rather than ridership on a household or zonal basis.

One of the simplest research designs to implement is the basic *before-and-after design*, as represented in table 3-2. In interpreting the figure, assume that the household is to be the unit of analysis (each household constituting one case), and that the program of interest is to be implemented in one or more target areas, at least during the initial year. The term *observation* indicates data collection involving whatever impact measures are appropriate, while the term *treatment* represents the operation of the program. The diagram moves in time from left to right; thus this first design involves the collection of baseline data before the program is started, then the implementation of the program, followed by a second round of data collection at a time when the program's intended effects would be expected to have materialized. Obviously, the length of time between the two sets of observations depends on the substance and time frame of the program design; the "after" observation may come midstage during a continuing program or after the program is completed.

As applied to a formative evaluation, the postprogram observation in the before-and-after design would occur at the end of an appropriate period of programmed activity; the program would continue in operation beyond that point, and hopefully evaluative feedback would improve performance in the future. More important to the essence of a truly formative evaluation, however, is the idea of developing an understanding of the "whys and wherefores" of observed program performance, explanations of *how* the program operates as it does with an eye toward developing recommendations for improving performance. In this regard, it is important to recognize

Table 3-2
Before-and-After Design

Target areas:	Observation	Treatment	Observation

that the "observation" in table 3-2 and subsequent research designs usually represents not a single data point but rather the collection of a data set including multiple indicators. In a formative evaluation, this set of observations includes process measures as well as impact indicators in order to facilitate the analysis of linkages which may go a long way toward explaining these reasons for program success or failure.

An advantage of this design over the *one-shot case study* (postprogram observations only) is that it provides a way of measuring actual change over time. The impact condition—rates of compliance with building codes or burglary rates, for example—is observed across all the households or a sample of households in the target area before and after the program has been in operation in order to determine whether this impact condition has improved during the course of the program.

With good impact indicators, this should be sufficient to indicate whether or not the intended impacts have occurred, but the before-and-after design is not a strong approach for isolating the underlying cause-effect patterns. If a positive change or impact is noted, it may well be the result of the program as anticipated. However, it is possible that it could also be the effect of some coincidental change in environmental factors. The before-and-after design has no way of distinguishing between these two possibilities. If there is no plausible rival explanation, if all relevant environmental factors have been monitored over the same time period and no shifts which could explain the impact have been noted, then the evaluators can conclude with some confidence that the program did in fact produce results. However, there is always the possibility that some environmental factors of which the evaluators are unaware are actually responsible for the change in impact conditions.

A variation of the before-and-after design would be to have more than one postprogram observation, perhaps measuring effects during, immediately after the program's completion, and then at some interval after program completion in an area in order to assess immediate, short-range, and longer-range impacts. While this approach might be appropriate, depending on the substance of the program and its intended time frame, it still does not counteract the possibility that some environmental factor, as opposed to the program intervention, might be responsible for the observed changes.

A further expansion of this type of noncomparison design is the extended *time-series approach*, as shown in table 3-3. In time-series analysis, observations are taken at multiple points in time prior to program implementation and are continued during and after program operation. The major purpose of this approach is to establish trends, if any, that were developing in the impact condition before the program implementation in order to determine whether the postimplementation observations deviate substantially from what would have been expected on the basis of past trends.

Table 3-3
Time-Series Design

Target areas:	Obs.	Obs.	Obs.	Obs.	Obs.	Treatment	Obs.	Obs.	Obs.	Obs.	Obs.

Although table 3-3 refers to data being collected for multiple target areas, this design is basically a *single-time-series design* because it involves only observations that receive the same kind of program treatment. It is an improvement over the simple before-and-after design for evaluating certain types of programs precisely because it does consider changing levels of impact conditions over time before the program intervention. Thus, if impact conditions exhibit variation on a regular cycle, seasonal variation, for example, the evaluator can take this into account and sort out these effects from bona fide program effects. In general, analysis of the preprogram time series may be used to assess the degree of instability in the data from observation to observation and serve as the basis for determining whether a change observed from immediately before to after the program departs significantly from the magnitudes of increases and decreases that had been occurring in any case before the program was implemented. If such a change from before to after the program is observed, and if it appears to represent a direction or amount of change that would be unlikely to have occurred simply as a continuation of the observed past trends, it may well represent an impact of the program.

However, with this type of single-time-series design, the possibility still remains that although a relatively substantial change in impact condition did occur as intended by the program design, this change could still be the effect of some nonprogram influence. Thus the single-time-series design is most appropriate when the evaluator can be fairly confident that the environment will *not* be shifting in a way that could confound the analysis of program effects. If, for example, transit ridership had been falling off during the preprogram series and there is no indication of any environmental factors which might have changed that trend, an increase in ridership in the postprogram series could be attributed to the improvement program with a fair degree of confidence.

Comparison Designs

The ability to attribute observed effects to program treatments is greatly enhanced if the evaluation is based on the comparison of program areas with nonprogram areas. The most straightforward design along these lines is the *before-and-after comparison-group design* shown in table 3-4. The

Table 3-4
Before-and-After Comparison-Group Design

Target areas:	Observation	Treatment	Observation
Comparison areas:	Observation		Observation

relevant impact conditions are observed at the same time prior to program implementation in both program and nonprogram, or comparison, areas and then are repeated at the same time in both sets of areas after the program has been in operation. The basic logic of this approach is that if the areas are equivalent, and if the program is effective, the anticipated impacts should materialize in the target areas but not in the comparison areas.

If the intended impacts are found to have occurred in the target areas and not in the comparison areas, it may well be an indication that the program has indeed produced the desired results. However, the basic problem with this design is that there could be differences between the areas themselves that were responsible for the differences in observed effects. Could it be that the observed effects would have occurred in the target area even if the program had not been implemented, while it would not have occurred in the comparison areas in any case because of differences between the two areas?

The adequacy of the before-and-after comparison-group design rests on the degree to which the program and comparison areas are equivalent in terms of the factors that might influence program results or changes in impact conditions. The question really is: Do these areas in fact provide for *fair* comparisons? In selecting comparison areas, then, the important environmental variables should be taken into account as well as the impact conditions. For example, with respect to the housing-rehabilitation program, the areas should be comparable in terms of such factors as income, age of residents, and transiency, as well as the impact condition, percent of dwelling units which are not in compliance with building codes. Given the difficulty in finding areas that are truly comparable, a variation of the design which may be advantageous is simply to use more than one comparison area that may be comparable to the program areas in different respects. However, this approach is clearly weaker than having a comparison area that is truly comparable.

An additional feature that might be incorporated into this design if the program is to be continued in subsequent years and expanded to new areas would be the use of new areas first as comparison areas and then as target areas. In this *cyclical before-and-after comparison design*, shown in table 3-5, areas that can be targeted in advance as future program areas are used as comparison areas in the first cycle of the program, while in subsequent cycles they become target areas. Additional areas which never receive the

Table 3-5
Cyclical Before-and-After Comparison Design

Target area 1:	Obs.	Treatment	Obs.		a	a
Target area 2:	Obs.	Treatment	Obs.		a	a
Target area 3:	Obs.		Obs.	Treatment	Obs.	a
Target area 4:	Obs.		Obs.		Obs.	Treatment	Obs.
Target area 5:	Obs.		Obs.		Obs.		Obs.

aObservations may be repeated periodically.

program may or may not be included. In any case, this design is very efficient in terms of data collection because information which is first collected for comparative purposes can also be used to establish time-series data for areas which are brought into the program later on. First-year program areas may also be observed periodically after the program to examine long-range impact.

In addition to having a comparison area that is comparable in terms of the impact condition at the time period immediately preceding the program implementation, depending on the nature of the program being examined, it might well be advantageous to have comparison areas with similar trends in the impact variables across a longer time span before the program. This suggests the use of a *multiple-time-series design* with which such preprogram trends can be taken into account. As shown in table 3-6, the multiple-time-series design expands the single-time-series design by affording a comparison in time series between program and comparison areas.

With this approach, the preprogram time series can be compared, first of all, to determine whether the areas were in fact equivalent in terms of trends in the impact condition prior to the program. If these trends are found to be different, moreover, these preprogram series can be used to interpret similarities or differences in postprogram series. For example, if the postprogram series in both program and comparison areas are found to show a moderately decreasing trend in burglary rates, this might well represent an important finding if the preprogram series for the target areas had shown sharply increasing rates while the preprogram series for the comparison areas had shown steadily decreasing rates even before program implementation. Thus the multiple-time-series design often affords an improvement over the before-and-after comparison-group design, but the validity of multiple-time-series analysis still depends on the two sets of areas essentially being equivalent in terms of the relevant environmental variables. In the preceding example, for instance, if the target areas had also been the subject of increased routine police patrol while the comparison areas had not, the evaluator would not be able to sort out the possible effects of the crime-prevention program from the possible effects of the increase in patrol.

Table 3-6
Multiple-Time-Series Design

Target areas:	Obs.	Obs.	Obs.	Obs.	Obs.	Treatment	Obs.	Obs.	Obs.	Obs.	Obs.
Comparison area:	Obs.	Obs.	Obs.	Obs.	Obs.		Obs.	Obs.	Obs.	Obs.	Obs.

A variety of these lower-level designs are employed in the case studies presented in this book. The Harrisburg Housing-Rehabilitation Program is evaluated for the most part using a simple before-and-after design, while some aspects of the evaluation are based on the comparison-group design. Furthermore, as that program is implemented in other target neighborhoods, there may be an opportunity to extend the analysis using the cyclical before-and-after design. The other two cases utilize time-series approaches. The Williamsport Transit-Improvement Program evaluation relies on a single-time-series approach—repeated observations of the service area as a whole—while the York Crime-Prevention Program uses a multiple-time-series approach.

Summary

Developing a research design for any evaluation is a matter of fitting the characteristics of alternative designs to the specific purposes of the evaluation, the context in which the program was implemented, and the time, cost, and feasibility constraints on the evaluator. The designs employed in the case studies were selected in each case because they were thought to be capable of producing valid results in the specific context as well as being attractive from the point of view of data requirements and feasibility.

Notes

1. See Theodore H. Poister, *Public Program Analysis: Applied Research Methods* (Baltimore: University Park Press, 1978), chapter 3 for a more complete treatment of various types of measures and data sources.
2. See Harry P. Hatry et al., *How Effective Are Your Community Services: Procedures for Monitoring the Effectiveness of Municipal Services* (Washington: Urban Institute, 1977), for a thorough discussion of alternative measures and data sources for local program evaluation.
3. For thorough treatments of the design and conduct of citizen surveys, see Earl R. Babbie, *Survey Research Methods* (Belmont, Calif.: Wadsworth, 1973); and Eugene J. Webb and Harry P. Hatry, *Obtaining Citizen Feedback: The Application of Citizen Surveys to Local Governments* (Washington: Urban Institute, 1973).

4. See Edward A. Suchman, *Evaluative Research: Principles and Practice in Public Service and Social Action Programs* (New York: Russell Sage, 1967), pp. 115-126.

5. See Wesley G. Skogan, "Victimization Surveys and Criminal Justice Planning" *University of Cincinnati Law Review* 45(2), 1976, pp. 167-206; and Philip H. Ennis, "Field Surveys II: Criminal Victimization in the United States: A Report of a National Survey" (Washington: U.S. Government Printing Office, 1967) for a discussion of the need for victimization surveys; and Ann Schneider, *Measuring the Change in the Crime Rate: Problems in the Use of Official Data and Victimization Survey Data* (Eugene: Oregon Research Institute, 1975), for a discussion concerning the use of both official data and victimization surveys.

6. See Poister, *Public Program Analysis*, chap. 9; and Donald T. Campbell and Julian C. Stanley, *Experimental and Quasi-Experimental Designs for Research* (New York: Rand McNally, 1963), for more indepth discussions of research design.

7. See Carol H. Weiss, *Evaluation Research* (Englewood Cliffs, N.J.: Prentice-Hall, 1972), chapter 4; and Campbell and Stanley, *Experimental and Quasi-Experimental Designs*, chapters 1-3 and 7-15.

4

The Harrisburg Housing-Rehabilitation Program Design

Introduction

In the late 1960s and especially in the 1970s, rehabilitation of decaying neighborhoods has become a major strategy of housing assistance, developing in reaction to the mass clearance—new construction projects of earlier urban renewal efforts.[1] The Housing Act of 1965 provided low-interest loans and grants on a large scale for the rehabilitation of dwellings for targeted groups. A more comprehensive law, the Housing and Community Development Act of 1974, provided block grants to cities to support coordinated programs geared to improving community infrastructure and services. The act consolidates previously fragmented federal assistance programs such as urban renewal, codes enforcement, urban beautification, and housing rehabilitation to promote coordinated program efforts. The consolidation also granted cities more flexibility (as well as responsibility) in the use of Housing and Urban Development funding and allowed city governments to tailor programs to their specific needs.[2]

As a strategy, rehabilitation assumes that the social, as well as physical, structure of a neighborhood is worth maintaining and deemphasizes demolition and relocation efforts. The Housing and Community Development Act encourages local governments to approach the problems of inner-city residential neighborhoods with a comprehensive program that addresses the entire living environment, intended in part to stem the flight of wage-earning families from the inner-city areas. Thus the aim is to go beyond the provision of physically adequate shelter to affect the neighborhood itself. By emphasizing infrastructure and municipal service improvements in addition to structural renovation, rehabilitation centers on the goal of stabilizing transitional neighborhoods, those which have basically sound structures and have not yet been overwhelmed by deteriorating conditions.[3]

With the help of the Community Development Block Grant, officials in the city of Harrisburg, Pennsylvania designed and implemented a new program geared to stemming the physical and social decline of its older, once attractive residential neighborhoods. The housing-rehabilitation program incorporated several features designed to bring about substantial, measurable improvement in living conditions in the targeted areas.

Harrisburg, a city of about 58,000 population, has been faced with a decreasing population over the past two decades. As in other cities, many older residential areas represented a neglected asset that was in danger of becoming a liability to the city. As the problems of urban living multiplied, the decline of some neighborhoods was evidenced by increasing vacancy rates, more tax delinquencies, and government acquisition of deteriorated properties. The housing-rehabilitation program is aimed at revitalizing such neighborhoods, particularly those with sound housing stock and a solid basis for renovation.

Initially, two target neighborhoods were chosen specifically because they appeared to be appropriate for rehabilitation. They were not classified as blighted, but had the symptoms of neglect (for example, abandoned structures, rubbish in yards, broken down fences and porches, obsolete plumbing and electrical fixtures) and were expected to continue to decline without active intervention to reestablish the structures as attractive, safe dwellings and to improve the neighborhood's overall physical environment. The city hoped to reverse the trend of increasing neglect by working with owners to upgrade their properties, thereby stabilizing the condition of houses and preventing further deterioration throughout the target areas. By far the majority of houses in both target areas were occupied at the start of the program; no massive relocation effort or extensive rehabilitation of city-owned properties was involved in these neighborhoods. The program was designed to focus the city's efforts primarily on the designated areas for an unspecified period, then to expand, reaching out to other neighborhoods.

The city's main role was to provide the impetus and the means for owners to take it upon themselves to rehabilitate their dwellings. At the same time, the city planned to undertake complementary projects in the target areas to promote stronger, safer, more attractive neighborhoods for residents. These activities include community infrastructure improvements (for example, improved street lighting, repaired sidewalks, recreation areas, and street plantings), reduction of nuisances and safety hazards, and upgraded basic municipal services, such as police patrol and rubbish collection. In Harrisburg, the mounting of a program aimed at improving housing conditions was clearly in line with citizen priorities. A recent survey of Harrisburg residents showed that respondents thought the need for increased governmental efforts at improving existing housing structures through codes enforcement and reduction of nuisances and safety hazards was second only to the need for better crime prevention and law enforcement.[4]

In part because the Community Development Block Grant Program introduced the first HUD requirements for local evaluation of projects and activities undertaken by grantees,[5] the city of Harrisburg arranged to collaborate with university researchers on the housing-rehabilitation evaluation.[6] The intention was to develop an evaluation design which could be implemented and maintained for the most part on an inhouse basis.[7] City personnel were largely responsible for data collection, while the university researchers took the lead in the analysis. Throughout the process, however, from design through execution, the evaluation team worked closely with city personnel in an attempt to improve the city's own evaluation capabilities.

Program Design

As figure 4-1 shows, the Harrisburg Housing-Rehabilitation Program consists of four components, including (1) a systematic housing codes inspection coupled with (2) financial assistance to subsidize the costs of the repairs and improvements. Additional activities were designed to support the codes-inspection and rehabilitation components of the program, including (3) improvement of neighborhood infrastructure and (4) improved management of city-owned properties.

The primary objective of the housing-rehabilitation program is to upgrade all the residential properties in the target areas of the city. Specifically, the objectives of the housing-rehabilitation program are

To bring substandard dwelling units that are suitable for rehabilitation up to codes standards.

To eliminate public safety hazards and substantially reduce the rodent problem (vector control).

Beyond these immediate objectives, longer-range impacts were expected to result in the target areas. These are

A decrease in vacancy rates.

An increase in dwelling units that are owner-occupied.

A reduction in the outmigration of residents.

An improvement in citizen attitudes toward their neighborhoods.

An increase in property values.

A decrease in the number of tax-delinquent structures.

Underlying Strategy

Together, the four components of the housing-rehabilitation program make up a systematic program designed to meet the preceding objectives. This evaluation focuses on the two major components, regulation and rehabilita-

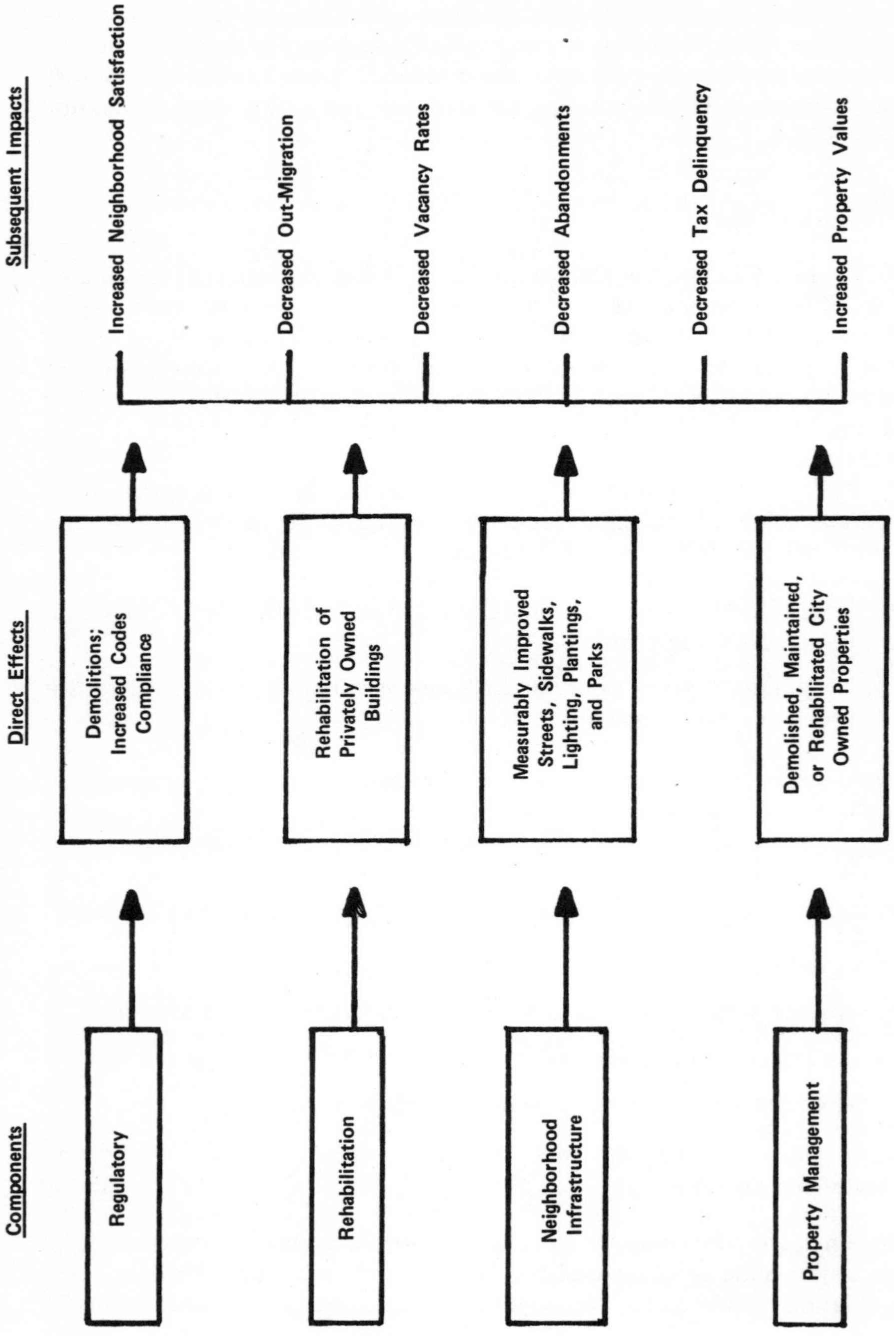

Figure 4-1. Harrisburg Community Development Program.

tion, although some of the preceding anticipated effects are at least partially dependent on implementation of all four components to have their fullest impact. Figure 4-2 displays the program logic, focusing on the two major components, regulation and rehabilitation. The figure indicates the specific elements, outputs, linking variables, and direct effects expected to result from the program. As the figure shows, the two components are linked together; the intended strategy was for the codes-inspection program to lead to owner participation in the rehabilitation program. This strategy is based on a "carrot and stick" approach, offering an incentive to bring a property into codes compliance (technical and financial assistance through the housing-rehabilitation component) and at the same time presenting an element of coercion (threat of legal action for continued noncompliance with codes). The initial codes inspection introduces the owner to the opportunity to take advantage of the rehabilitation program, and theoretically should encourage the owner to participate, bring the structure into compliance, and remove the threat of enforcement.

Regulatory Component. The main emphasis of the regulatory component is a program of codes inspection and follow-up activities in the target areas. Bureau of Codes Administration inspectors, working out of the site offices, note sanitation as well as building codes violations. If a property is initially in compliance, no further action is necessary. However, if the structure does not meet minimum housing-code requirements, the structure is cited for violations; the inspector determines if the house can be rehabilitated or recommends demolition. If the structure is suitable for rehabilitation, a detailed report of violations and estimated costs of repairs is sent to the owner. Also, the owner receives a letter explaining the city's housing-rehabilitation program and indicating the procedure to follow for obtaining financial assistance. If the property is found to be unfit for rehabilitation, acquisition and demolition steps are taken by the city.

Rehabilitation Component. The target-area site offices are headquarters for rehabilitation efforts as well as for the codes inspections. The program staff provides financial and technical assistance to property owners and reinspects properties after repair work has been done to ensure quality workmanship.

If a property does not meet codes requirements, the owner is introduced to the program's rehabilitation support activities. The owner is eligible, regardless of income, for a grant from the city to help pay the cost of home repairs. For owner-occupants, 25 percent of costs is reimbursable; for absentee owners, 15 percent; and for owner-occupants who are 62 or over or who are disabled, 40 percent is reimbursable. This grant is offered to help owners meet the costs of repairs and also as an incentive to have the work

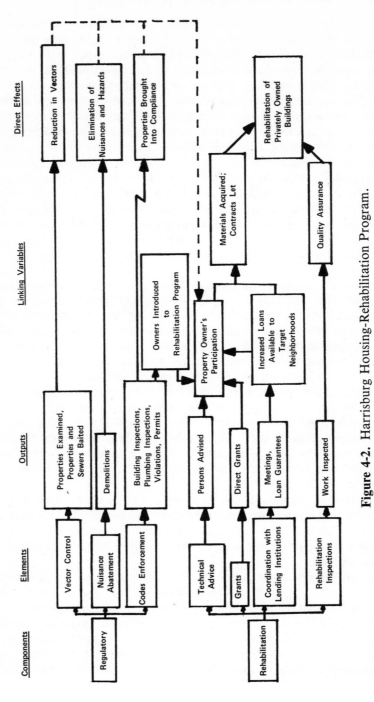

Figure 4-2. Harrisburg Housing-Rehabilitation Program.

done expediently while the grant program remains in effect. The reimbursement is made contingent on satisfactory inspection of the repairs.

An additional means of financial assistance was made available through the housing-rehabilitation program with the cooperation of local banks and savings and loan associations. Original expectations were that many owners would be unable to meet the costs for repairs and would require financing. Thus arrangements were made to ensure assistance from banks for property owners with acceptable credit ratings.

As part of the program, a mechanism was developed to review the cases of owners who could not quality for a homeowner's loan at participating financial institutions. A loan committee was established to (1) guarantee to a lending institution against default by the property owner—a hardship loan—or (2) recommend that no loan be granted. Upon authorization of a hardship loan, the full guaranteed amount would be put into an escrow account from the program funds.

Figure 4-3 is a flowchart of the main steps in the process from initial codes inspection through anticipated results. At the initial inspection, determination is made as to whether the house meets codes standards. If not, but if suitable for rehabilitation, it was expected that the owner would take advantage of the grant for improvements, and where necessary, the loan process. The flowchart shows the various paths leading to property rehabilitation and compliance. Other possible courses are continued noncompliance or demolition of the structure, if not suitable for rehabilitation.

Program Management

As a new approach to the problems of city neighborhood deterioration, implementation of the housing-rehabilitation program required difficult decisions about untried plans. The city's block grant application was approved and funds were available to initiate the program in the autumn of 1975. After the general concept of the program components had been developed, piecing out the details of program design and routine operations took quite a bit of time, and the gearing up phase of the program was slow to get under way. For example, although city officials had made successful initial contacts with financial institutions, the actual negotiations of the contracts for loan arrangements between the city and financial institutions were slow and took some time to complete.

Implementation. The original target areas encompassed a total of about 850 dwelling units in two separate residential neighborhoods of the city. Allison Hill, with a predominantly white population, has mostly row houses. In the Uptown area, with a large nonwhite population, semidetached houses predominate.

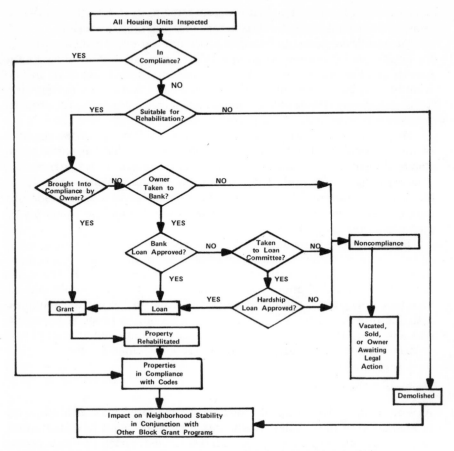

Figure 4-3. Property Disposition through Rehabilitation Process.

By October 1975, site offices were set up in the target areas and codes inspections began. Public meetings in the neighborhoods, media publicity, and letters to property owners explained the program and the procedures that would be followed. The proactive vector-control element of the program was never initiated in the target areas, although there is a general citywide effort at vector control on a complaint basis. Reduction of safety hazards through increased demolitions of properties unsuitable for rehabilitation was undertaken to some extent, in conjunction with codes inspection of properties.

Concurrently with the implementation of the regulatory and rehabilitation components, neighborhood infrastructure improvements were undertaken in the target areas. Tree planting, improved street lighting, a children's park, and sidewalk repairs were among the initial improvements. The Bureau of Property Management undertook the task of rehabilitating several city-owned structures in the target areas prior to placing them on the market for sale. Most other city-owned properties in the target areas are not suitable for rehabilitation and have been or will be demolished. In May 1976 the target areas were expanded to include blocks adjacent to the initial areas, and a second expansion followed in June 1977. Plans for further expansion of the program had not been made as of autumn 1977.

In the initial areas, the first phase of the program began to wind down in mid-November 1977, about two years after its inception. After that date, property owners who had not taken advantage of the financial assistance were no longer eligible to participate; those already participating could receive reimbursement for rehabilitation projects begun before the cutoff date. The next phase of the program calls for reinspection of properties not brought into compliance and subsequent strict codes enforcement. At the time of the evaluation, the codes-inspection and rehabilitation parts of the program continued to operate in the expansion areas.

Administration. Designed by officials in the Department of Community Development and the mayor's office, the housing-rehabilitation program operations take place at the two target-area site offices, with support from city hall. Many of the initial major decisions were made jointly, and decisions were carried out by staff in the Bureaus of Planning and Codes Administration within the Department of Community Development. Initially, the codes administrator was responsible for the gearing up of the program in the target areas. Within the first year of operation, city officials thought there was a need for better organization and direction of the program. At that point, a program coordinator was hired to oversee the program. The program coordinator position was filled from autumn 1976 through late spring 1977, during which time the coordinator reported directly to the mayor. At the time of the evaluation, Bureau of Codes Administration and Bureau of Planning personnel have shared the responsibility for directing and monitoring the program. Target-area supervisors report to the codes administrator and provide data for program evaluation to a planner in the Bureau of Planning.

The mayor and his staff and Bureau of Planning staff were active in determining the types of neighborhood improvements to be implemented. Thus there was no one decision maker responsible for the design and implementation of neighborhood infrastructure improvements. According to one city official, many of the needs in the target areas were obvious. As the program evolved, other decisions were made jointly by the mayor and department and bureau heads as the needs arose. Such decisions included the time and extent of expanding the target areas and the time to end the first phase in the initial target areas and begin strict codes enforcement.

Evaluation Strategy

The evaluation of the Harrisburg Housing-Rehabilitation Program was designed and implemented as an integral part of the program design. Working together, city officials and university researchers developed the evaluation strategy, tailoring it to the specific features of the Harrisburg program. The basic approach and steps in developing the evaluation, however, are applicable in other small and medium-size cities and with other programs.

Although the HUD block grant requirements specified the inclusion of follow-up reports for monitoring purposes, the planners of the Harrisburg program initially had no model to follow in developing their strategy for an effectiveness evaluation. Effectiveness evaluations of similar programs in other cities have not been widely reported.[8] The approach taken here is essentially straightforward, but as will be seen, the interpretations are not always clearcut. This evaluation examines the regulatory and rehabilitation components, the core of the broader revitalization effort. The major hypotheses to be tested relate to the direct effects and subsequent impacts expected to result from the program. These include

An increase in rehabilitated properties.

An increase in the demolition of public safety hazards.

A decrease in tax delinquency.

An increase in property values.

A positive change in citizen attitudes about their city government.

Improved residents' attitudes about their neighborhoods.

Research Design

In order to adequately evaluate the housing-rehabilitation program, a research design with varied strategies was developed. Based on the type of available measures, this "patched up" design utilizes a case-study approach, a before-and-after comparison, and a comparison-group design. The case study focused on the program process itself, tracing the evolution and outputs of the regulatory and rehabilitation components according to the sequence shown in figure 4-3. The before-and-after portion examined variables external to the program that might be expected to show change over time in the target areas as a result of the program. Inclusion of a comparison neighborhood allowed further analysis of variables external to the program which also apply to areas of the city not included in the program.

This combination of different types of comparisons makes the overall research design stronger than any single aspect alone. City planners attempted to select a comparison area with demographic characteristics as similar to the two target areas as possible. There were difficulties in finding an appropriate comparison area for several reasons. First, there are significant differences between the two target areas, so an appropriate comparison area for one might not be appropriate for the other. In general, the selection of two comparison areas matched to the two program areas would have been a preferred strategy, but because of time and money considerations, this was not done. A second problem was to find an area in which no other housing or neighborhood improvement program was in effect. Such programs would negate the attempt to make a fair assessment of the housing-rehabilitation program. Since several other residential areas of the city were involved in such improvement programs, the selection was necessarily limited. Finally, the search for an adequate comparison area was frustrated by the fact that each neighborhood is in some sense unique. The two target areas in this program were chosen precisely because they had certain characteristics which indicated a need for the program as well as some potential for program success; there may be no other areas with the same set of critical characteristics. Therefore, the strategy must necessarily be to use an approximate comparison area and modify interpretations accordingly. At the time the comparison area was selected, it was considered as a possible candidate for future expansion of the housing-rehabilitation program. Although no specific data on the condition of properties were available for comparison with the target areas, the comparison area appeared to have a substantial proportion of well-maintained properties as well as some abandoned buildings and deteriorated structures. It includes more single-family dwellings than do the target areas, which have more semidetached and row houses. In terms of racial composition, the nonwhite population in the comparison area is greater than that in one of the target areas and smaller than that in the other area.

Measures and Data Sources

The evaluation employs various types of data, including program-operation data, secondary data from city hall and elsewhere, and primary survey data. As much as possible, assessment of program activities relied on routine data collected for use in day to day operations. This type of data traced the progress of the program, indicating program outputs such as number of initial housing inspections completed, number of structures initially in compliance/violation, number of loans authorized, and number of demolitions recommended. These outputs represent steps in reaching program objectives. According to the program logic, the combination of outputs should lead to the intended direct effects (for example, increase in number of structures in compliance with housing codes) and subsequent impacts.

At first the program data were maintained at the site offices but not organized in a manner suitable for monitoring the program over an extended time period. The evaluation team recommended that monthly reporting forms be instituted in order to facilitate the evaluation. These forms consolidated information on outputs and activities at the site offices, focusing primarily on the types of indicators previously mentioned. Also, recap sheets were maintained on each property, detailing the progress from initial inspection to final status. Together, the recap sheets and the monthly reporting forms were designed to monitor site-office activities; a copy of each form is included in appendix B. Although these reporting forms were meant to streamline the process of collecting data for analysis, they were found to have inconsistencies and gaps (the result of misunderstandings of their intended use and the differences in procedures between the two site offices), and their reliability may be questioned.

City records provide another source of data for the evaluation. These include information on building and demolition permits, property transactions, and tax delinquencies. These data differ from program operation data in that they are not restricted to the duration and boundaries of the housing-rehabilitation program. Because these records cover a longer period of time, before-program data can be used as a benchmark against which to compare after-program data. This allows measurement of change; for example, a substantial increase in the number of building permits issued to property owners in the target areas might represent a high rate of housing-improvement activity prompted by the rehabilitation program. Decrease or stabilization in the tax-delinquency rate, available from city hall, would indicate a relative increase in the city's tax revenues from the target areas.

Transaction prices for properties sold over the last several years were thought to represent a fair measure of change in property values,[9] but although the data are available, they are difficult to interpret. Many factors which cannot adequately be accounted for influence transaction prices. External demand for properties, general economic and inflation trends, and the number of similar properties available can affect a sale price. Also, purchase of tax-delinquent properties for low prices and sales of property between family members will affect the average sale price of properties in an area without reflecting actual market value.

If property transaction prices are to be used as an indicator of change in property values, they must be used with caution. In fact, this indicator could be very misleading, masking the positive effects of the housing-rehabilitation program. For example, if the program has the effect of (1) encouraging responsible owner-occupants to repair their houses and stay in the neighborhood because of improved neighborhood conditions, and at the same time (2) encouraging owners of extremely delapidated but rehabilitable houses to sell their properties rather than face threats of codes enforcement, the average selling price of houses might be expected to decrease. Also, people might be more willing to purchase an inexpensive house in a target area and take advantage of the financial assistance to repair the property themselves. Thus the indicator would not reflect the positive impact of the program in the short run.

Data from these secondary sources are useful for another reason. Not only do they allow comparisons over time, but they also can be used to compare target areas with no-program areas elsewhere in the city. Thus using the example of building permits, the change in rate of permits issued can be compared over the same time period for the program and comparison areas. If the increase in building permits issued is evident in a comparison area as well as in a program area, then the increase cannot be attributed to the implementation of the program. If, on the other hand, the comparison area did not show a similar increase in building permits, that would lend support to the assumption that the program indeed spurred applications for building permits.

The third type of data used to evaluate the housing-rehabilitation program was obtained in a postimplementation survey of one of the target areas and the comparison area. In the target area, a similar survey was undertaken prior to the program implementation; the results from the two surveys provide before and after information on residents' attitudes toward their neighborhood. In addition to the measure of change within the target area, comparison in attitudes can be made between the comparison area and the target area in an after-only-with-comparison design. Although it is a one-shot survey, some of the questions asked respondents to indicate their opinions of changing neighborhood conditions over time, for example, is the neighborhood deteriorating, is crime increasing, are people taking better care of their homes than they were two or three years ago? This type of question was intended to give some idea of residents' perceptions of change in their neighborhood and would apply equally to the target area and the comparison area.

Notes

1. For a discussion of the development of housing rehabilitation as an assistance strategy, see Harry J. Wexler and Richard Peck, *Housing and*

Local Government (Lexington, Mass.: Lexington Books, 1975), pp. 100-104; and David Listokin, *The Dynamics of Housing Rehabilitation* (New Brunswick, N.J.: Center for Urban Policy Research, Rutgers University, 1973), pp. 6, 8.

2. See Arthur Naparstek et al., *Neighborhood Reinvestment: A Citizen's Compendium to Programs and Strategies* (National Center for Urban Ethnic Affairs, 1977), for an overview of the Housing and Community Development Act of 1974 and other public and private approaches to neighborhood reinvestment. See also the United States Department of Housing and Urban Development's annual reports on the Community Development Block Grant Program.

3. See William Gorham and Nathan Glazer (eds.), *The Urban Predicament* (Washington: Urban Institute, 1976), pp. 3-5 for an overview of federal housing strategy.

4. Theodore H. Poister, James C. McDavid, and Susan K. Miller, *A Report of Harrisburg Residents' Evaluations and Preferences for Local Governmental Programs and Services* (University Park: Institute of Public Administration, Pennsylvania State University, 1976).

5. Office of Evaluation, Community Planning and Development, United States Department of Housing and Urban Development, *A Guide for Local Evaluation* (Washington, June 1975).

6. See Theodore H. Poister, James C. McDavid, and Anne H. Magoun, *Applied Program Evaluation for Small and Medium-Size Cities* (University Park: Institute of Public Administration, Pennsylvania State University, 1977).

7. Theodore H. Poister and Charles L. DeBrunner, *Harrisburg Community Development Program Evaluation Design: Working Paper No. 1* (University Park: Institute of Public Administration, Pennsylvania State University, 1976); Charles L. DeBrunner and Theodore H. Poister, *A Design for Housing Program Evaluation in York, Pennsylvania* (University Park: Institute of Public Administration, Pennsylvania State University, 1977).

8. Reports on the Block Grant Program published by HUD generally discuss the various approaches cities have taken in implementing their programs. These reports show aggregate trends, useful for monitoring purposes, and focus on a few selected cities for more thorough discussion. However, they do not represent the type of formative evaluation discussed in this book. See, for example, United States Department of Housing and Urban Development, *Community Development Block Grant Program, Third Annual Report, 1977* (Washington: U.S. Superintendent of Documents, 1977).

9. See Roger S. Ahlbrandt, Jr., and Paul C. Brophy, *Neighborhood Revitalization* (Lexington, Mass.: Lexington Books, 1975).

5 Evaluation of the Housing-Rehabilitation Program

Introduction

The evaluation of the housing-rehabilitation program examines data in light of the hypotheses outlined in the previous chapter. As a formative evaluation of an ongoing program, the intention was to analyze the program operation, effects, and subsequent impacts in order to assess how well the program is meeting its objectives and to suggest possible modifications for the future as the program expands into new areas.

The discussion of the findings traces the program through operational data, then evaluates the direct effects of the program and subsequent impacts. Attitudinal data from surveys as well as program and secondary data are included. Generally, the discussion of the program process focuses on the initial target areas (labeled Allison Hill and Uptown in the tables) because it was assumed that any effect would be most likely to appear in the areas where the program has been in operation the longest. Where this is not the case, it is specified in the text. The data do not cover the entire period of program operation, even in the initial target areas. Unless otherwise indicated, data collection is complete through mid-November 1977.

Program Implementation

Table 5-1 shows the results of initial codes inspections in the two target areas. It is obvious that in both areas almost every structure had been inspected, that the systematic codes-inspection element of the program was implemented. The following discussion pertains to those houses which have been inspected.

As shown in table 5-1, on initial inspection, most properties in both target areas were not in compliance with housing and/or sanitation codes. The initial compliance rate was higher in Allison Hill, where there were also fewer sanitation violations reported. Although there may be differences in the inspection procedures carried out at the two site offices, it is unlikely that this would account for the broad differences in proportions of sanitation- and housing-codes violations. Overall the table shows that both areas were feasible targets for a housing-rehabilitation program.

Table 5-2 indicates for each area the initial inspection status according

Table 5-1
Status of Dwelling Units in Initial Inspection

Initial Status	Allison Hill Number	Percent	Uptown Number	Percent	Total Number	Percent
In compliance	121	25.4	20	5.9	141	17.3
Noncompliance—codes	338	70.9	221	65.6	559	68.7
Noncompliance—sanitation	3	0.6	9	2.7	12	1.5
Noncompliance—both	6	1.3	82	24.3	88	10.8
Missing	9	1.9	5	1.5	14	1.7
Total	477	100.1	337	100.0	814	100.0

Source: Site-office files.

to the occupancy status of the structure. The table does not show much of an association in either area. However, because of a high rate of missing data on occupancy status (particularly for properties initially in compliance) in Allison Hill (42 percent), the results may be biased. The data for Uptown are more complete, with information on 93 percent of the properties in the area, and still show only slight association. In Uptown, vacant structures were most likely to be cited for sanitation- and housing-code violations.

Table 5-3 shows, for each area, the estimated cost of rehabilitation by occupancy status. Estimated cost is used here as an indicator of the degree to which owners have maintained their properties in good condition; the lower the estimated cost, the better condition the property is in. In both areas, owner-occupied units have the smallest proportion of high estimated costs, $1,000 or more, and vacant units have the highest proportion of high estimated costs. Theoretically, the codes inspectors note estimated cost of repairs in their files for all structures that are in violation of codes. In fact, the estimated cost was calculated only in some cases. Once again the figures for Uptown are more complete than for Allison Hill.

The absence of data in so many cases raises the question of whether adequate efforts were made to introduce the program to owners and to interest them in rehabilitating their properties. The inspectors were often the first and only personal contact property owners had with program staff, and their initial explanations of the program could be expected to have a real influence on owners' attitudes and decisions of whether or not to participate.

The large amounts of missing data also raise the issue of the validity of this indicator because it is difficult to determine what the estimated cost figures really represent. Data on estimated costs from site-office files may not accurately represent the total estimated cost of complete repairs needed to bring a structure into codes compliance; for instance, in some cases con-

Table 5-2
Status of Dwelling Units in Initial Inspection by Occupancy Status

Initial Status	Owners		Renters		Vacant		Total	
	Number	Percent	Number	Percent	Number	Percent	Number	Percent
Allison Hill								
In compliance	16	8.7	2	2.8	1	4.3	19	6.8
Noncompliance—codes	166	90.2	67	94.4	18	78.3	251	90.3
Noncompliance—sanitation	1	0.5	—	—	2	8.7	3	1.1
Noncompliance—both	1	0.5	1	1.4	2	8.7	4	1.4
Missing	—	—	1	1.4	—	—	1	0.4
Total	184	99.9	71	100.0	23	100.0	278	100.0
Uptown								
In compliance	11	5.9	3	3.7	—	—	14	4.5
Noncompliance—codes	129	68.6	55	67.9	30	66.7	214	68.2
Noncompliance—sanitation	5	2.7	2	2.5	—	—	7	2.2
Noncompliance—both	43	22.9	21	25.9	15	33.3	79	25.2
Total	188	100.1	81	100.0	45	100.0	314	100.1

Source: Site-office files.

Table 5-3
Estimated Cost of Rehabilitation of Dwelling Units by Occupancy Status

Estimated Cost	Owners		Renters		Vacant		Total	
	Number	Percent	Number	Percent	Number	Percent	Number	Percent
Allison Hill								
$100 or less	6	6.5	1	3.6	—	—	7	5.3
$101-500	30	32.3	6	21.4	3	30.0	39	29.8
$501-1,000	30	32.3	7	25.0	1	10.0	38	29.0
$1,001-5,000	27	29.0	13	46.4	5	50.0	45	34.4
$5,001 or more	—	—	1	3.6	1	10.0	2	1.5
Total	93	100.1	28	100.0	10	100.0	131	100.0
Uptown								
$100 or less	5	3.3	1	1.5	—	—	6	2.3
$101-500	28	18.3	4	6.1	2	5.0	34	13.1
$501-1,000	41	26.8	13	19.7	5	12.5	59	22.8
$1,001-5,000	74	48.4	47	71.2	25	62.5	146	56.4
$5,001 or more	5	3.3	1	1.5	8	20.0	14	5.4
Total	153	100.1	66	100.0	40	100.0	259	100.0

Source: Site-office files.

tractor bids were used to estimate costs of repairs, but the bids might cover only a portion of the required work to be done, with the rest to be done by the property owner. Had the inspectors estimated costs for the entire repair needs, as was initially intended, the results would not only be more complete, but they also would be more valid as indicators. Because of the large amount of missing data, the results may be biased, yet the pattern is similar for both areas. The general finding (which is more clear in the Uptown data) would be expected; owner-occupants take better care of their properties than do absentee landlords, and at least some of the vacant units were probably uninhabitable because of the dilapidated condition of the structure.

It was originally anticipated that most property owners would apply for bank loans to help them meet the costs of rehabilitating their houses. In fact, as table 5-4 shows, only a small number of property owners have taken advantage of the loan options. Rather than go into debt, many property owners have chosen to do the repair work piecemeal, receiving reimbursement for work already done before beginning another task. This has allowed them to pay for work as it is done, stretching the work and payments over a longer period, but avoiding interest payments. Based on this information, it would seem that the loan provisions were well intentioned but *not* a particularly suitable mechanism for these neighborhoods. However, where a property owner did go through the loan process, it appears that the city-guaranteed loans were utilized to an appreciable extent, particularly in the Uptown area. Thus the program designers were correct in their assumption that a proportion of loan applications would be rejected by financial institutions; in that respect, the hardship-loan provisions did help make funds available to those who wanted to take advantage of a loan.

Table 5-5 indicates the expenditure of funds on program activities in the initial target areas through September 1977. Here again it is obvious that Uptown property owners have spent more through loans (bank and hardship) and that Allison Hill owners have spent more through private savings, using the reimbursements from the city. Although there are more participants in Allison Hill than in Uptown, total expenditures are greater in

Table 5-4
Loan-Provision Utilization

	Allison Hill	Uptown	Total
Number of bank loan recipients	5	11	16
Number of persons rejected by banks	7	26	33
Number of hardship loan recipients	3	20	23

Source: Bureau of Planning, Department of Community Development, *Cumulative Activity Update through September 1977.*

Table 5-5
Program Expenditures: Initial Program Areas

	Allison Hill	Uptown	Total
Total reimbursements	$ 46,145.00	$ 41,313.00	$ 87,458.00
Private rehabilitation loans (bank)	6,986.00	13,338.00	20,324.00
Private rehabilitation loans (hardship)	2,471.00	37,849.00	40,320.00
Private rehabilitation savings	103,551.00	82,605.00	186,156.00
Total	$159,153.00	$175,105.00	$334,258.00

Source: Bureau of Planning, Department of Community Development, *Cumulative Activity Update through September 1977.*

Uptown. Overall, the expenditure level is much lower than previously anticipated. For the first program year, $450,000 was available to be spent on grants and loans in the target areas. Two years later, this amount still had not been spent.

Site-office data files and reimbursement records were used to analyze participation in the housing-rehabilitation program by estimated cost of rehabilitation. There is not a clear pattern, but table 5-6 shows that the highest rate of participation was where the estimated cost was between $100 and $500. In Allison Hill, 73.9 percent of property owners with estimated costs of $100 to $1,000 have received reimbursement, indicating participation in the program, but only 54.3 percent of those with estimated costs of more than $1,000 received reimbursements. In Uptown, the data show a lower overall rate of participation, with less than one-half of those for whom data were available receiving reimbursement. It must be cautioned here that the data may be biased, particularly in the case of Allison Hill, where there is a large amount of missing data on estimated costs. Since estimated cost was frequently calculated on the basis of contractor bids submitted after the initial inspection, such bids would be more likely to be in the files for eventual program participants than for nonparticipants. Files from Allison Hill may have contained more contractor bids than did those from Uptown, thus distorting the proportion of houses out of compliance that participated in the program.

Effects on Code Compliance

The major objective of the housing-rehabilitation program was to increase the number of properties in compliance with housing codes. In order to more fully assess the effect of the program, current status of structures initially out of compliance was cross-tabulated with the estimated costs of

Table 5-6
Participation in Program by Estimated Cost of Rehabilitation[a]

Participation	$100 or less		$101-500		$501-1,000		$1,001-5,000		$5,001 or more		Total	
	Number	Percent	Number	Percent	Number	Percent	Number	Percent	Number	Percent	Number	Percent
Allison Hill												
Yes	4	50.0	42	73.7	40	74.1	38	59.4	–	–	124	65.6
No	4	50.0	15	26.3	14	25.9	26	40.6	6	100.0	65	34.4
Total	8	100.0	57	100.0	54	100.0	64	100.0	6	100.0	189	100.0
Uptown												
Yes	1	14.3	12	35.3	15	25.4	33	21.9	4	26.7	65	24.4
No	6	85.7	22	64.7	44	74.6	118	78.1	11	73.3	201	75.6
Total	7	100.0	34	100.0	59	100.0	151	100.0	15	100.0	266	100.0

Source: Site-office files and Department of Community Development Reimbursement Records through mid-September 1977.
[a]Based on records of reimbursements to participants.

rehabilitation. The results show whether there is an association between the extent of repairs needed (as measured by estimated cost of repairs) and the current compliance status. Table 5-7 suggests that there may be a modest association, with a smaller proportion of owners with high estimated costs ($1,000 or more) bringing their properties into compliance. Because the associations are not strong, and because of large amounts of missing data, this table should be interpreted with caution. If in fact this table does represent the change in compliance status in the target areas, it would indicate that the program was more successful in rehabilitating structures that needed less expensive repairs than the properties in very bad condition.

The pattern is suggested even more strongly in the No Work category. The percentage of properties with high estimated repair costs rises substantially in both target areas. There are so few cases of estimated costs of $100 or less that it is difficult to interpret them. (The seeming contradiction between the Participation figures in table 5-6 and Progress to Date figures in table 5-7 may be explained in one of two ways. In a few cases, owners have had work done or made repairs themselves without requesting reimbursement. Another possible explanation for the higher No Work figures (table 5-6) than the No Work figures (table 5-7) is that work may have been started but reimbursement not yet processed at the time of data collection.)

The assessment of program effects attempted to measure any association between the initial compliance status and occupancy status of dwelling units. However, the data show no meaningful association between initial status and whether the dwelling was owner-occupied, renter-occupied, or vacant.

One of the most obvious patterns observed in the data analysis is shown in table 5-8. Simply stated, people eligible for the higher reimbursement categories (25 or 40 percent) were more likely to bring their properties into compliance with codes than were those in the 15 percent eligibility category. In Allison Hill, 61.0 percent of older or handicapped property owners whose properties initially were not in compliance with codes brought their homes up to codes standards, but only 28.6 percent of younger owner-occupants and 23.8 percent of absentee landlords did so. The same pattern is evident in the Uptown data. Interpretation of these results should consider the extent of repairs required to rehabilitate properties. It could be that the greater level of reimbursement is a significantly greater incentive, or that the absentee landlords are not interested in rehabilitating their properties, or that there is a systematic difference in the level of repairs required for the different categories of eligible owners which affects their desire and/or ability to pay.

The success of the rehabilitation program in bringing houses up to codes standards can best be measured overall with the available data by determining the change in codes status from the time of the initial inspection to the

Table 5-7
Progress to Date by Estimated Cost of Rehabilitation of Dwelling Units

Progress to Date	$100 or less		$101-500		$501-1,000		$1,001-5,000		$5,001 or more		Total	
	Number	Percent	Number	Percent	Number	Percent	Number	Percent	Number	Percent	Number	Percent
Allison Hill												
Compliance–codes	3	37.5	27	52.9	31	58.5	30	48.4	1	16.7	92	51.1
Compliance–sanitation	—	—	—	—	—	—	—	—	—	—	—	—
Compliance–both	—	—	—	—	1	1.9	—	—	—	—	1	0.6
Work in progress	2	25.0	15	29.4	12	22.6	11	17.7	—	—	40	22.2
No work	3	37.5	9	17.6	9	17.0	21	33.9	4	66.7	46	25.6
Demolished	—	—	—	—	—	—	—	—	1	16.7	1	0.6
Total	8	100.0	51	100.0	53	100.0	62	100.0	6	100.1	180	100.1
Uptown												
Compliance–codes	5	71.4	10	29.4	14	23.7	23	15.2	—	—	52	19.5
Compliance–sanitation	—	—	—	—	5	8.5	7	4.6	—	—	12	4.5
Compliance–both	—	—	—	—	2	3.4	4	2.6	1	6.7	7	2.6
Work in progress	1	14.3	15	44.1	14	23.7	41	27.2	4	26.7	75	28.2
No work	1	14.3	9	26.5	24	40.7	67	44.4	4	26.7	105	39.5
Demolished	—	—	—	—	—	—	9	6.0	6	40.0	15	5.6
Total	7	100.0	34	100.0	59	100.0	151	99.9	15	100.1	266	100.0

Source: Site-office files.

Table 5-8
Progress to Date by Eligibility Category for Reimbursement

Progress to Date	15 Percent		25 Percent		40 Percent		Total	
	Number	Percent	Number	Percent	Number	Percent	Number	Percent
Allison Hill								
Compliance–codes	20	23.8	30	28.6	36	61.0	86	34.7
Compliance–sanitation	–	–	–	–	–	–	–	–
Compliance–both	1	1.2	–	–	–	–	1	0.4
Work in progress	17	20.2	26	24.8	14	23.7	57	23.0
No work	45	53.6	48	45.7	9	15.3	102	41.1
Demolished	1	1.2	1	1.0	–	–	2	0.8
Total	84	100.0	105	100.1	59	100.0	248	100.0
Uptown								
Compliance–codes	12	17.4	16	22.9	19	51.4	47	26.7
Compliance–sanitation	5	7.2	2	2.9	–	–	7	4.0
Compliance–both	4	5.8	2	2.9	1	2.7	7	4.0
Work in progress	20	29.0	32	45.7	10	27.0	62	35.2
No work	28	40.6	18	25.7	7	18.9	53	30.1
Demolished	–	–	–	–	–	–	–	–
Total	69	100.0	70	100.1	37	100.0	176	100.0

Source: Site-office files.

end of the first phase of the program. Table 5-9 shows initial and up-to-date codes status for Allison Hill and Uptown. In both cases, the data are almost complete, ensuring representative results. In Allison Hill, a total of 28.1 percent of properties that were originally in violation of codes have been brought up to housing-code standards, and in Uptown, 19.5 percent have been brought into compliance. When sanitation codes are also considered, the Allison Hill figure barely changes, but in Uptown, the percentage increases to 29.0 percent, which is similar to the Allison Hill compliance figure. In Uptown, there is a greater proportion of properties where work is in progress (25.9 percent of properties initially in violation of codes), whereas in Allison Hill, there is a larger proportion (51.6 percent) of properties with no work reported. Including properties that were initially in compliance, the up-to-date compliance rate is still only about 47 percent for Allison Hill and 33 percent for Uptown.

The bias or distortion in the data in table 5-9 should be limited. The No Work figure may be overstated if owners had taken steps to have work done just prior to data collection but the site office personnel had not yet recorded it. Because owners were notified that the first phase of the program was near an end in the initial target areas, it is likely that some who had not gotten around to making repairs earlier would have chosen to take advantage of the program during the last weeks. If anything, of course, such activity would indicate more positive effects of the program than are shown in table 5-9.

Because the city does not maintain records on citywide codes-compliance rates (compliance status is usually determined on a complaint-only basis), it is difficult to measure how Allison Hill and Uptown compare with the rest of the city, or even with the comparison area in terms of codes compliance. Within the target areas, however, the change in compliance status can be measured. As table 5-10 shows, in Uptown, where originally only 20 structures were in compliance, now 88 meet housing-code standards, an increase of 340 percent. The change is not as dramatic in Allison Hill, where intially there were 121 properties in compliance. The present rate represents an increase of about 84 percent, to a total of 223 structures in compliance. If all work-in-progress properties are brought into compliance, the overall housing compliance rate for Uptown would reach 57.0 percent, just over half the properties in the area. The same rate would be 60.0 percent for Allison Hill.

The number of building permits issued by the city represents another type of measure of program effects. Because the building-permit records are maintained independently of the housing-rehabilitation program, they are available on a citywide basis and for preprogram years. As an external indicator of program performance, building-permit information can be used to help determine first of all, whether there was, in fact, an increase in build-

Table 5-9
Progress to Date by Original Status for Dwelling Units Out of Compliance

Progress to Date	Noncompliance, Codes		Noncompliance, Sanitation		Noncompliance, Both		Total	
	Number	Percent	Number	Percent	Number	Percent	Number	Percent
Allison Hill								
Compliance–codes	96	28.7	–	–	1	14.3	97	28.1
Compliance–sanitation	–	–	–	–	–	–	–	–
Compliance–both	–	–	–	–	2	28.6	2	0.6
Work in progress	61	18.2	–	–	2	28.6	63	18.3
No work	175	52.2	2	66.7	1	14.3	178	51.6
Demolished	3	0.9	1	33.3	1	14.3	4	1.4
Total	335	100.0	3	100.0	7	100.0	345	100.0
Uptown								
Compliance–codes	59	26.6	–	–	2	2.4	61	19.5
Compliance–sanitation	–	–	7	77.7	16	19.5	23	7.3
Compliance–both	–	–	–	–	7	8.5	7	2.2
Work in progress	56	25.2	–	–	25	30.5	81	25.9
No work	91	41.0	2	22.2	32	39.0	125	39.9
Demolished	16	7.2	–	–	–	–	16	5.1
Total	222	100.0	9	99.9	82	99.9	313	99.9

Source: Site-office files.

Table 5-10
Present Status of Dwelling Units

	Allison Hill		Uptown		Total	
	Number	Percent	Number	Percent	Number	Percent
Originally in compliance	121	25.4	20	5.9	141	17.3
Brought into compliance—codes	100	21.0	61	18.1	161	19.8
Brought into compliance—sanitation	—	—	23	6.8	23	2.8
Brought into compliance—both	2	0.4	7	2.1	9	1.1
Work in progress	63	13.2	81	24.0	144	17.7
No work	186	39.0	129	38.3	315	38.7
Demolished	5	1.0	16	4.7	21	2.7
Total	477	100.0	337	100.0	814	100.1

Source: Site-office files.

ing or rehabilitation activities in the target areas (complementing the program-operations data) and second, if such an increase could be attributed to the existence of the program. By using data for the comparison area, the evaluators could control for the possibility of rival hypotheses which might have caused an increase in the number of permits issued. The 1973 and 1974 building-permit data cover completely no-program data years, data for 1975 include only about two months of program activity, and 1976 and 1977 are program years. Building permits are required for any work with estimated costs of $500 or more, so the indicator should be consistent for all three areas. Table 5-11 shows building-permit data for the initial and expanded target areas and for the comparison area. It is obvious that the number of building permits issued in Allison Hill and in Uptown has increased dramatically, but that there has been only a slight increase in the comparison area. In 1977, 57 permits were issued in Allison Hill and 99 in Uptown, a further increase over the 1976 figures. During the same time period, only one building permit was issued in the comparison area. If the comparison area really is relatively similar to the two target areas in other respects, it can be said that the housing-rehabilitation program is having a strong effect in encouraging people to make extensive improvements to their properties, that is, that the properties would not have been rehabilitated without the rehabilitation program. This finding supports the hypothesis that the program, not some external factor, was responsible for the increased building structure activities and subsequent increase in compliance with codes rate.

In addition to increasing the rate of codes compliance, the other immediate objective was to reduce or eliminate the number of public safety hazards. The number of demolitions in the target areas can serve as an indicator of this objective. Because of time and money constraints, demolition figures were not collected for this evaluation. These are, however, available from the Bureau of Codes Administration and, like the building-permit data, can be compared with preprogram years and with the comparison-area demolition statistics. It is reasonable to assume that the demolitions ordered by the city are indeed public safety hazards. This is particularly

Table 5-11
Building Permits Issued, 1973-1977

	1973	1974	1975	1976	1977
Allison Hill	7	6	11	59	57
Uptown	2	8	17	71	99
Comparison Area	0	2	5	8	1

Source: Building permit records, Bureau of Codes Administration.

true over the past couple of years when the cost of demolitions has increased to the point that even extensive rehabilitation is often less expensive in the long run than is demolition.

Subsequent Impacts

The subsequent impacts hypothesized to occur as a result of the housing-rehabilitation program include a decrease in tax-delinquency rates, an increase in property values, reduced vacancy rates and increased neighborhood stability, and improvement in residents' attitudes toward their neighborhood and toward the city's efforts to improve the neighborhood. At the time of the evaluation, the program had been in effect in the initial target areas for about two years, not long enough to measure long-term impacts with certainty. Although the time frame is too short for a thorough analysis, the method of evaluation in terms of tax delinquency, property values, and citizen attitudes is worthwhile. Vacancy rates and outmigration of residents can be investigated later on with the use of postal surveys and the school census.

Table 5-12 illustrates the number and percent (of total structures) of tax delinquencies in the two target areas and the comparison area from 1971 to 1977. Structures are considered to be tax delinquent if taxes have not been paid by the end of the calendar year. There is no apparent relationship between the institution of the housing-rehabilitation program and tax-delinquency rates. Although tax delinquencies in the comparison area increased at a faster rate than in the target areas, the trend is quite similar in all three areas. However, continued observation of the areas may show changes that develop over a longer period. The value of using a comparison

Table 5-12
Tax-Delinquency Rates

Year	Allison Hill		Uptown		Comparison	
	Number	Percent[a]	Number	Percent	Number	Percent
1971	4	0.8	2	0.6	4	0.6
1972	6	1.3	5	1.5	5	0.7
1973	6	1.3	8	2.4	14	2.1
1974	17	3.6	16	4.7	20	3.0
1975	44	9.2	31	9.2	80	11.8
1976	69	14.4	60	17.8	149	22.0
1977	59	12.3	51	15.1	114	16.8

Source: Tax office records, city hall.

[a]Represents percent of total number of structures in the area which are tax delinquent for one year.

area is highlighted by the data in table 5-12; without the comparison area, the temptation might be to attribute the slight decrease in delinquency rates in the target areas from 1976 to 1977 to the program without considering possible external influences. Since the same pattern appeared in the comparison area as well, it is doubtful that the rehabilitation program played a major role in the decrease in tax delinquencies.

The mean property transaction prices (1970 through 1977) for the target areas and the comparison area are shown in table 5-13. As mentioned earlier, change in mean property value must be viewed circumspectly because of possible influencing factors that have not been accounted for. Size and condition of structure, dwelling type, and location affect the selling price, as do such things as economic conditions, city migration figures, and relative supply and demand for properties. Also, the prices in table 5-13 may be misleading because they do not indicate constant dollars for year to year comparisons. Another point to stress is that the properties sold may not be representative of their neighborhood property values; for example, they may be in better than average condition and therefore attractive and high priced, or they may be sold cheaply at sheriff's auction for an extremely low bid. In the latter case, the low price may induce a buyer to invest in the property and rehabilitate it to increase the value. In such instances, the existence of the housing-rehabilitation program may encourage people to buy otherwise unsalable properties. Also, interpretation of transaction prices must take into consideration the general instability in the trend over time. Because there was no obvious pattern prior to the program, the change in a given year or two could very well occur by chance.

At this point, it must be concluded that mean transaction prices do not support the hypothesis that the program has led to a measurable increase in property values. However, in Allison Hill the number of transactions has

Table 5-13
Mean Property Transaction Prices

Year	Allison Hill		Uptown		Comparison	
	Price	Number	Price	Number	Price	Number
1970	$8,273	20	$7,852	21	N/A	
1971	$5,879	30	$7,071	22	N/A	
1972	$5,906	31	$9,347	24	N/A	
1973	$5,981	31	$8,286	9	$8,845	24
1974	$6,789	39	$9,814	21	$9,461	31
1975	$5,406	23	$6,889	17	$9,852	23
1976	$6,276	27	$9,483	15	$7,141	12
1977	$7,542	17	$4,711	15	$9,072	30

Source: Deed transfer records, city engineer.

decreased since the program's initiation; this may indicate a new trend toward a more stable neighborhood with fewer property turnovers. If such a trend develops and is not replicated in no-program areas, more detailed analysis of property transactions—beyond simple sale prices—may reveal whether or not the program has an effect on property values and neighborhood stability. Data to evaluate would include condition of the property at time of sale and occupancy status before and after sale. As with tax-delinquency-rate data, it would be important to consider rival hypotheses.

Neighborhood Perceptions

In 1975, before the initiation of the housing-rehabilitation program, the city's Bureau of Planning conducted a survey of residents in the Allison Hill area. The questionnaire focused primarily on citizens' attitudes toward their neighborhood and their concerns for municipal services improvement. The evaluation team fielded a similar survey, replicating some parts of the initial questionnaire, in October 1977. This provided a before-and-after program-implementation comparison for Allison Hill. The second survey was also fielded in the comparison area so that attitudes between the two areas could be compared on a one-time basis. To help evaluate perceptions of change over time, some questions asked respondents to indicate impressions of change (in level of crime, in housing conditions, etc.) in their neighborhood over the past several years. Also, homeowners in the target area were asked several questions relating to the housing-rehabilitation program. The survey questionnaire is in appendix B.

Before-and-After Comparison

The 1975 survey had responses from 249 individuals in Allison Hill, and the 1977 survey had 300 responses from the same area. There were an additional 161 responses from the comparison area. Analysis of the Allison Hill data did not show any appreciable change in attitudes from 1975 to 1977. In fact, where change was evident, it tended to be slightly negative. Although more respondents in 1977 indicated positive attitudes about area recreational facilities, fewer agreed that the neighborhood is a good place to bring up children. Attitudes toward housing conditions were somewhat more negative in the 1977 survey. In order to provide for a fair comparison, respondents to the 1977 survey who had been in the neighborhood for two or more years were selected as a subsample to determine how their attitudes compared with the first survey results. Again, there was little discernible change on most questions. Overall, the results of this before-and-after comparison suggest that, in spite of the improvement in rate of codes compliance and the neighborhood infrastructure improvements, the program has not had a noticeable effect on residents' attitudes toward their neighborhood, with the exception of evaluations of street lighting. It is possible that over time such a change will become apparent.

Comparisons with No-Program Area

The second type of survey comparison was between the program area (which covered the first expansion as well as the initial Allison Hill target area) and a no-program area. The purpose of the comparison was to determine whether the program-area residents appear to have attitudes different from those in similar areas that have not had the program. While in the aggregate, the comparison area was appropriate for analysis of such variables as tax delinquencies and property transactions, closer inspection suggested that part of the area was markedly different from the Allison Hill target area. In that section, houses were in better condition, properties were well-maintained, and in general the neighborhood seemed to be better off than the other half of the larger comparison area. Responses to the 1977 survey confirmed that only about one half of the original comparison area was well-matched to the target area in terms of demographic characteristics, with the exception of racial composition. Thus in order to provide a fair comparison, the analysis of the survey data was limited to responses from the appropriate part of the comparison area and an area adjacent to the Allison Hill target area (also a candidate for expansion of the program) for a no-program comparison. Table 5-14 illustrates the demographic characteristics of the target (program) area and the no-program area as they were represented in survey responses. The similarities on all counts except race are apparent. Because of the difference in racial composition of the two subsamples, the analysis controls for race to see if that environmental variable may have been an influencing factor in shaping respondents' attitudes.

A discussion of the highlights of the 1977 survey follows. The responses to statements with which respondents were asked to agree or disagree have been dichotomized, including "neutral" with the response that indicates a more negative attitude. The effect of this was to bias results against the positive response, perhaps understating the positive attitudes in both program and comparison areas. The responses are shown in appendix B.

City Commitment to Improving Neighborhood. One of the hypotheses examined in the evaluation is that the implementation of the housing-

Table 5-14

Demographic Characteristics of Survey Sample by Area

Characteristic	Program		No Program	
	Number	Percent	Number	Percent
Length of time in neighborhood:				
1 year or less	32	14.1	18	11.4
2-5 years	45	19.8	29	18.4
6-10 years	27	11.9	22	13.9
11-15 years	19	8.4	19	12.0
16-20 years	24	10.6	26	16.5
21 or more years	80	35.2	44	27.8
Total	227	100.0	158	100.0
Race:				
White	185	82.6	92	57.9
Nonwhite	39	17.4	67	42.1
Total	224	100.0	159	100.0
Age:				
15-20 years	9	4.0	11	6.9
21-35 years	57	25.2	38	23.9
36-50 years	38	16.8	30	18.9
51-65 years	54	23.9	40	25.2
66-90 years	68	30.0	40	25.2
Total	226	99.9	159	100.1
Annual income:				
$5,000 or less	56	30.6	40	33.6
$5,000-$10,000	57	31.1	34	28.6
$10,000-$15,000	35	19.1	26	21.8
$15,000-$20,000	18	9.8	8	6.7
$20,000 or more	17	9.3	11	9.2
Total	183	99.9	119	99.9
Dwelling type:				
Single family	5	2.2	9	5.8
Semidetached	34	15.2	85	55.2
Row house	169	75.8	40	26.0
Apartment building	15	6.7	20	13.0
Total	223	99.9	154	100.0

rehabilitation program would improve residents' attitudes about the city's commitment to improving their neighborhood. Although there are no preprogram data on this question to evaluate change over time, it is obvious that program-area residents are more likely to think that the city is committed than are residents of the no-program area. Table 5-15 shows the breakdown of responses to this statement for the program and no-program areas, controlling for race. Overall, 65.0 percent of the program-area residents but only 25.4 percent of no-program-area residents agreed with that, and there was virtually no difference between the responses of whites

Table 5-15
"The City Government Is Committed to Improving the Quality of
this Neighborhood"

	Program		No Program		Total	
	Number	*Percent*	*Number*	*Percent*	*Number*	*Percent*
Total						
Disagree	68	35.1	94	74.6	162	50.6
Agree	126	64.9	32	25.4	158	49.4
Total	194	100.0	126	100.0	320	100.0
Whites						
Disagree	55	34.8	53	76.8	108	47.6
Agree	103	65.2	16	23.2	119	52.4
Total	158	100.0	69	100.0	227	100.0
Nonwhites						
Disagree	13	36.1	41	71.9	54	58.1
Agree	23	63.9	16	28.1	39	41.9
Total	36	100.0	57	100.0	93	100.0

and nonwhites in the different areas. This result strongly supports the
hypothesis that the program has an effect on people's perception of the city
government.

Attitudes about the Neighborhoods. Although in the aggregate it appears
that there is no difference between the program and no-program areas with
respect to attitudes about housing conditions (about 40 percent in each
agreed that housing is in good condition), nonwhites in the program area
were more likely to agree that housing is in good condition than were nonwhites in the comparison area. The reverse was true to a lesser extent for
whites.

Housing. Overall, a minority in both areas agreed that housing conditions
have improved in the past couple of years, but more in the program area
than the no-program area agreed with this. Also, in the program area,
slightly over half the respondents agreed that people take better care of their
homes than they did two or three years ago, slightly more than the percentage who agreed in the no-program area. The pattern for nonwhites showed
more agreement in the no-program area than in the program area. Along
the same lines, a minority of respondents in both areas agreed that properties are well maintained, but more agreed in the no-program area than in the
program area. However, more than half the nonwhites in the program area
agreed with the statement, reversing the overall pattern.

Respondents were asked if they would rather stay in their neighborhood or move. Generally, the proportion of responses from the program-area respondents is about equally divided, but more no-program-area respondents would choose to stay. More than one-half the nonwhites would choose to stay than to move, particularly in the no-program area. Overall, respondents tended to think that market value of properties has decreased or stayed the same over the last few years. However, the proportion of respondents in the program area who thought the market value increased is greater than in the no-program area. Abandoned houses were not perceived as a problem by the majority of respondents in either area. The program-area respondents considered abandoned buildings less of a problem than did those in the no-program area, and they were less likely to think that the number of abandoned buildings had increased in the past couple of years.

Generally, the responses to questions on housing do not show a distinct pattern of difference between the program area and the no-program area. From this part of the survey, it would be difficult to say that the attitudes of program-area residents are more positive toward housing conditions than those of no-program-area residents.

Neighborhood Infrastructure. Respondents in the program area were very much aware of the well-lighted streets, showing a great contrast with the respondents of the no-program area. Also, overall, more program-area respondents than no-program-area respondents agreed that streets and sidewalks were in good condition. This pattern was quite evident for whites, but reversed for nonwhites.

Recreational Facilities and Children. Although more program-area respondents than no-program-area respondents thought the neighborhood had good recreational facilities, a smaller proportion in the program area thought that the neighborhood was a good place to bring up children. Overall, the majority disagreed with both statements. Differences between whites and nonwhites in response to these questions reduced the extent of difference between the two areas.

Overall Satisfaction. Questions about overall satisfaction with the neighborhood indicated that, in general, respondents in the program area were more likely to agree that their neighborhood was deteriorating than were respondents in the no-program area. On the other hand, there was almost no difference between the areas overall on the question of whether the neighborhood is becoming a better place to live. Generally most respondents disagreed with that statement, but nonwhites in the program area disagreed somewhat less frequently than nonwhites in the no-program area.

Conclusions and Recommendations

Conclusions

For the most part, the housing-rehabilitation program has been implemented as planned, although the funds have not been spent nearly as quickly as anticipated, and the loan provisions have been utilized only to a marginal extent. Also, the rate of participation by homeowners and the number of properties brought into compliance are lower than might have been expected. It can be said that the direct effects of the major components of the program have been achieved to a considerable extent, with an increase in the number of rehabilitated properties and a reduction in the number of eyesores and safety hazards. In addition, the neighborhood infrastructure has been improved with the addition of better street lights and other improved facilities.

On the other hand, the results in the target areas to date do not reflect an entirely successful program. More than one-half the properties remain unrehabilitated, and only about 30 percent of those initially in need of repair have been brought into compliance with codes. This low level of owner interest and cooperation suggests at least a partial failure in program or logic.

The program has been underway for two years, providing time to assess the implementation of the program elements and outputs. While there has been sufficient time to get the program in operation, the desired response has not always followed. This raises the question of how well the program was introduced to potential participants and whether adequate and appropriate follow-up procedures were instituted to encourage participation. During the 1977 survey, informal discussions with respondents sometimes revealed a lack of information or misinformation about the nature or procedures of the housing-rehabilitation program. There was some confusion about eligibility to participate and the options for financial assistance. The perceptions of some homeowners suggest misunderstandings and possibly reveal a reason for lower than expected participation. One possible conclusion here is that there has been a partial failure in program implementation which could well affect the results.

Beyond the problems with program implementation, it is worthwhile to examine the logic behind the program. It was assumed that the combination of systematic initial codes inspections with a report of violations to the owner along with the financial assistance options would provide enough impetus to stimulate owners' participation and rehabilitation of properties. Perhaps this was not sufficient to motivate people to action. The 1977 survey respondents who were eligible to participate (homeowners with codes violations) were asked if they participated and if not, why. Their answers suggest that for some people the expense was too great and they did not want to go into debt, or that they did not think they should have to repair relatively minor things while others in the neighborhood who had properties in much worse condition were doing nothing about rehabilitating them. Others indicated that they just were not interested in getting involved with the city's program and did not want to be told how to care for their properties. A frequent response from owners was that they just had not gotten around to doing anything about the repairs. Such responses challenge the assumption that the program logic is strong enough to stimulate owner participation.

When asked how the housing-rehabilitation program might be improved, the most frequent suggestion was to follow through with enforcement of the housing codes, requiring all homeowners to take steps to rehabilitate or maintain their properties. This type of response indicates that residents are aware of the need for improvement of properties in their neighborhoods and look to the city to do something about the problems. Perhaps the program logic would be stronger if it included provisions for systematic reinspections of properties and subsequent enforcement measures.

It is not possible to measure indirect or subsequent impacts with certainty at this time, but they should be monitored as the program continues. Interpretations will be more meaningful with more data. Citizens' attitudes about their neighborhood are still somewhat negative and do not appear to have improved since the program was implemented. There seems to be little difference between the program-area residents and residents of a comparison area in attitudes toward housing conditions in their neighborhoods. Residents' perceptions of the neighborhood infrastructure do show a difference between the program and the no-program areas. Overall, program-area residents were aware of the improved street lighting and recreational facilities and were more likely to think their sidewalks and streets were in good condition. Attitudes toward the city government's involvement in the neighborhood are very favorable in comparison with a no-program area.

The question of whether anticipated subsequent impacts, such as reduced vacancy rates, reduction in demolitions, and increased property values, will be achieved must consider the possibility that although the program has been implemented and is operational, perhaps the critical mass required to set in motion the subsequent impacts and spinoff benefits has not been reached. A realistic assessment of the program at this point cannot determine whether (1) more time is needed for subsequent impacts to be measurable, or (2) the passage of time will not show meaningful changes because of faulty program logic, or (3) the passage of time will not show meaningful changes because a critical mass has not been reached to spur the longer-range impacts.

Recommendations

The recommendations suggested by this evaluation relate to modifications in program operations which would strengthen the overall program and, hopefully, encourage greater participation among property owners.

1. A reinspection and codes-enforcement plan should be implemented during the time that financial and technical assistance are available to owners rather than as a separate phase of the program. Survey responses show that many residents are concerned about the deteriorating structures in their neighborhoods and would applaud codes enforcement.

Apparently, a one-shot systematic inspection of properties is not enough to encourage many property owners to rehabilitate their structures. The minimal effort for an enforcement plan would be reinspection of properties which were initially out of compliance. Presently, reinspections take place only after repair work has been done as a quality control measure before the city makes a reimbursement. A systematic reinspection of all properties initially out of compliance would show continuing concern on the part of the city government. Subsequent measures for enforcement of codes should be considered; these would be primarily the institution of financial penalties for continued noncompliance. The approach to such enforcement should depend on the nature and severity of the violations, with the overriding concern to be the establishment of living conditions which do not present health or safety hazards to occupants or the neighborhood.

Introduction of an enforcement program would implement the "stick" part of the "carrot and stick" philosophy that underlies the program logic. A visible enforcement effort in the initial program areas at this time may help convince owners in the expanded areas of the value of participating while financial assistance is available.

2. Program operation could be improved by establishing priorities understood by inspectors and property owners. By emphasizing the spirit rather than the letter of the codes, attention to certain types of major violations would be stressed. Then a homeowner would be faced with a list of significant problems as well as minor violations and encouraged to repair the big problems—those creating health or safety hazards—first. Such prioritizing of codes violations would be reflected in ensuing enforcement standards; heavier penalties would apply to more serious violations.

3. The publicity surrounding the initiation of the program in a new area should stress the entire process of rehabilitating properties. Because the loan provisions have not been heavily utilized, it is important to stress the availability of grants and procedures to follow in obtaining them, not emphasizing the loan provisions.

4. Codes inspectors should provide itemized estimated costs of repairs to the owner as part of the feedback following initial inspection. One of the

intended features of the program was close personal contact with property owners to introduce them to the program and to suggest how to bring their houses into compliance with codes. The inspectors should provide estimated costs for all priority violations at least, and in general should be thorough in their dealings with property owners. Real "hands on" treatment at this stage may result in greater participation. Because there is such great variation in the costs of improvements, such as the installation of a new furnace, the inspector should stress that the estimated costs reflect only a reasonable figure for standard repair work and that individual circumstances may vary considerably. This type of discussion of estimated costs, emphasizing the importance of giving priority to the major structural repairs, helps to coordinate the elements of technical and financial assistance and reflects the linkage between the regulatory and rehabilitation components as developed in the program logic.

5. The administration of the program could be improved by having a single person responsible for program operation. This has begun to happen under the new codes administrator, but lack of continuity of authority has created confusion at the site offices and in the record-keeping system. Changing policies may also have contributed to the confusion evidenced by some homeowners.

6. The office hours at the site offices could be adjusted so that they could be open more often in the evening when residents are likely to be at home. For homeowners who work during the day, evening hours provide the opportunity for visits to the site offices to take care of business. For those who have not gotten around to having work done or have had the work done but have not submitted receipts for reimbursement, the more convenient office hours might be a real benefit.

7. Participation might be increased if the financial incentives were greater. The present rate of reimbursement categories could be increased, still requiring the homeowner to shoulder most of the burden of rehabilitation, but with more governmental assistance. This option should be considered in expanding the program to new areas.

8. It is also recommended that since the program is continuing and is likely to be expanded into other areas of the city, evaluation efforts continue to monitor the progress of the program and its effects over time.

6 The Williamsport Transit-Improvement Program Design

Introduction

One of the biggest problems facing the new administration which took office in the city of Williamsport, Pennsylvania in January of 1976 involved the city-owned bus system. The system had been acquired by the city in 1969 when the private enterprise which had been operating it for years threatened to go out of business, leaving the area with no form of public transportation other than taxi service. This action ensured the preservation of transit service in the area, and the acquisition of new buses and other capital facilities and equipment—along with the availability of money from the city's general fund to help finance operations—permitted some initial improvement in service levels. Suburban jurisdictions which were provided service by the city's system contributed funds to help cover operating deficits, and the system received substantial financial assistance from both the federal Urban Mass Transportation Administration (UMTA) and the Pennsylvania Department of Transportation (PennDOT).

However, this proved to be a short-term solution to the area's public-transportation problems. Following national trends,[1] ridership on the Williamsport system continued to decline in the late 1960s and early 1970s, and while this trend was reversed in many Pennsylvania cities and areas in other parts of the country around 1973, the problem of increasing costs and decreasing ridership worsened in Williamsport during the period from 1973 through 1976. The most pronounced indication of the deteriorating performance of the transit system occurred when management made a very substantial reduction in the amount of service provided which was *not* followed by a decrease in operating costs, as should be expected. This reduction in service level was closely followed, however, by a fare increase aimed at generating increased revenue, but the combined impact of this service reduction/fare increase was a 14 percent decrease in total passengers from 1974 to 1975.

By 1976 it was clear that the system's performance levels were unacceptably low, but it was not so clear as to the reasons why or what could be done to improve the situation. PennDOT and UMTA, which were both providing operating subsidies to the system, were putting pressure on the city to find ways of increasing ridership while holding the line on costs. Some members of the city council, on the other hand, were beginning to promote the idea of abandoning the system or finding a way to turn it over to a separate authority. Finding himself in the middle of this issue, the mayor, who was generally service oriented, committed his administration to a policy of working to improve the overall performance of the system.

The situation Williamsport found itself in during this period was quite similar to that characterizing the state of public-transportation service in a great many U.S. cities. Typically, the pattern has been for private operators to go out of business or to be bought out by a public authority or general governmental unit which then injects new capital, equipment, and facilities into the system in an attempt to maintain or upgrade service levels.[2] While ridership losses have often been slowed down or even reversed, over time costs and operating deficits have increased dramatically to the point where local communities must face the issue anew of whether the system is worth retaining. To a great extent, however, decisions to discard local transit systems have been staved off by fairly generous financial support from UMTA and many state-level transportation departments.[3] The kind of systematic planning and evaluation illustrated here, conducted as part of a continuing and comprehensive multimodal transportation planning process, is a basic eligibility requirement for such federal financial support.

This set of circumstances gave rise to an evaluation of the existing system and related conditions and a planning effort to develop recommendations for improving service. After these recommendations—concerning a completely new service plan as well as improved management practices—were fully implemented, they became the focus of a follow-up study the next year intended to assess their impact. Thus, taken together the two studies constitute an evaluation-plan-reevaluation effort which has produced a considerable amount of information feedback that has been critical in terms of improving transit service in the Williamsport area. Both studies were designed and conducted as part of the Williamsport Area Transportation Study (WATS), an ongoing comprehensive multimodal transportation planning process involving state, federal, and local participation. The transit evaluation and planning work was done by a project staff including the city's planning director, transit manager, traffic engineer, and deputy director of finance in addition to an outside consultant.

The Original Study

Given the existing problems with internal management of the Bureau of Transportation, as evidenced by high rates of absenteeism, poor driver morale, and slipshod maintenance work, the original study concentrated on management as well as operations. This portion of the study produced recommendations concerning driver supervision, maintenance procedures, personnel changes, and information systems, most of which were put into practice during 1977. An additional product of the study was a five-year capital-improvement program including new buses, shelters, bus-stop signs, and maintenance equipment.[4] The major emphasis of the study, however, and that aspect which is of primary interest here, concerned the development of a new service plan aimed at improving the service provided to existing riders and making the system more attractive in order to generate increased ridership.

To get at the reasons why the operating system was performing poorly, the study employed several complementary approaches. First, an examination of the existing route network showed that there was a substantial duplication of effort in some corridors while other areas received inadequate service. Furthermore, on some routes, the buses ran only every 45 minutes or at hourly intervals, clearly an unacceptable level of service. Second, a procedure was established for organizing operating data routinely collected on the buses in order to facilitate route-by-route comparisons of certain operating statistics and performance measures. This analysis led to the identification of stronger and weaker routes in terms of utilization and the ratio of earned revenue to estimated operating costs, and it also showed that in terms of vehicle miles per vehicle hour there was a substantial slack on some routes, that is, slower average speed than necessary, and excess "layover time" when the buses were not in motion—all in all a significant underutilization of resources.

In addition to this secondary data analysis, four major primary data collection efforts were undertaken. One was the responsibility of the city's traffic engineer, who rode several buses on each route, noting any difficulties in operations, travel times between selected points, and in particular the degree to which arrivals and departures deviated from the printed schedule times. A second type of observational survey was a boarding and alighting survey, conducted on every run made during one single day, in which onboard observers counted the numbers of passengers getting on and off the bus at each stop. Analysis of the tabulated data showed which portions of the route network were most heavily traveled and revealed considerable "dead mileage" on certain routes, that is, stretches where the buses were consistently operating with few or no passengers aboard.

The single most important source of information was an onboard rider interview survey, also conducted on a 100 percent sample of passengers using the system during one entire day. A copy of the questionnaire used in this survey is included in appendix C.[5] It is designed to obtain data about the individual trip—origins, destinations, walking distances, etc.—and data about the way passengers rate the system and the kinds of improvements they think are necessary. This survey, which was filled out by the passengers with assistance from onboard distributors if necessary, garnered a 65 percent completion rate. A major emphasis of the analysis of these data involved the examination of current origin-destination patterns.

Table 6-1 shows transit-trip interchanges between pairs of geographic sectors; most of these sectors are combinations of adjacent transit-analysis zones. For example, the table shows that on the day of the rider survey there were an estimated 117 trips originating in the area known as Newberry and bound for the central business district (CBD), and another 99 trips going from the CBD out to Newberry. Examining the volumes of travel flows was the primary basis for determining priorities for routes which would directly connect various sectors together.

In addition to surveying passengers and their travel patterns, it was considered important to survey the community at large on a number of issues. For this purpose, a random sample of households in the service area was selected, including households located in all the outlying jurisdictions in addition to those in the city of Williamsport. This community survey was conducted by telephone, using a bank of telephones at the local civil defense installation, and yielded 959 completed interviews for roughly a 60 percent response rate. The respondents were asked a number of questions about

Table 6-1
Transit-Trip Interchanges

Origin Zone	Garden View	Newberry	Reach Road	West Side	Third Street	North Side	CBD	East Side	Penn Vale	Golden Strip	Montoursville	Duboistown	S. Williamsport	Total
Garden View	–	1	–	–	7	2	8	–	–	–	–	–	–	19
Newberry	3	28	9	32	36	5	117	9	10	10	10	–	1	271
Reach Road	–	3	–	9	8	–	20	8	–	1	8	–	2	60
West Side	2	20	3	44	24	3	206	11	6	28	14	1	8	376
Third Street	2	44	11	24	9	7	63	23	4	22	20	–	10	239
North Side	3	–	–	4	9	1	83	1	–	4	3	1	2	107
CBD	14	99	17	164	70	57	19	192	55	70	81	17	77	932
East Side	1	9	3	30	24	8	157	30	4	8	–	–	2	276
Penn Vale	–	8	–	7	4	8	58	13	7	2	1	–	1	109
Golden Strip	3	8	–	9	17	4	44	8	–	21	13	–	–	127
Montoursville	–	9	4	17	21	2	79	8	–	24	17	2	2	184
Duboistown	–	–	–	3	2	0	20	–	–	1	–	2	13	40
S. Williamsport	–	3	4	5	11	3	57	6	3	8	–	1	27	128
Total	28	232	50	354	241	96	931	309	89	200	166	25	146	2,868

Destination Zone

their household characteristics and travel patterns, including the extent to which members of the family used the bus system, the way they would rate the bus service at present, and whether they might be induced to using it or using it more if service were improved in various respects. In addition, they were asked about their views as to whether the bus system should be continued as is, reduced, eliminated, or expanded, and which unit of local government—the city, county, or a separate authority—should be responsible for operating it.

The overall set of results from these various data-collection efforts showed that there was indeed room for improvement of the public-transit system and that in the main, community sentiment was in favor of a public commitment to maintain and upgrade this service. More specifically, the data showed that in addition to the duplication of service on some routes and dead mileage and slack time on others, some residential zones within the service area were receiving only marginal service, while respondents to both the rider survey and the community survey indicated certain activity centers, particularly commercial areas, as desired destinations which were not presently accessible by bus. In addition, the infrequent service on some routes and inconvenience in transferring between certain pairs of routes were cited by both groups as detracting from greater ridership. Probably the most important general finding was that the existing route network was not very well aligned with some of the major flows in the overall trip-making pattern. Many trips whose origins and destinations were recorded by the rider survey could be made only very indirectly or with time-consuming transfers between routes in the downtown business district.

The Transit-Improvement Program

The detailed findings briefly summarized above suggested a complete revision of the service plan aimed at improving service levels with existing resources. Thus the major emphasis of the planning effort was the development of a new set of routes and schedules which would target service in greater conformity with observed travel patterns of present users and the expressed desires of both users and nonusers. The procedural objectives for developing the new routes and schedules were

> To increase the areas served by transit to cover important employment, commercial, and industrial centers not already served and improve service to residential areas considered to have potential transit demand.

> To improve major origin-destination connections and reduce the need for transfers through more direct routing and the use of through-routing.

To consolidate routes without reducing coverage by eliminating existing duplications of service and improve service levels without substantially increasing vehicle hours.

To establish 30-minute headways on all routes.

To provide two-directional service on all line-haul route segments and all corridors producing substantial transit trip making.

The overriding substantive objective which these improvements aimed to achieve was to maintain or increase transit ridership without incurring a corresponding increase in operating costs. More specifically, the overriding objective of the new system was determined to be

To achieve a 10 percent increase in total ridership on the system within one year of implementation without associated increases in costs beyond the normal toll of inflation.

Several alternative route alignments were proposed for various sectors of the service area, and various composite route networks for the entire area were developed using basic principles of system design such as through-routing, looping, or branching.[6] These alternatives were compared in terms of area coverage, directness of service, and convenience of transfers, as well as operational feasibility and the elimination of duplicated services. The primary criterion for evaluating the worth of a proposed route or combination of routes was the reduction of door-to-door travel time in the major flows of transit ridership. This operational criterion was based on the logic that since travel time is a very noticeable aspect of service quality and one which is important to people in determining *whether* to make a trip or *how* to make a trip, improving travel times would be a primary strategy for increasing ridership.

The Service Plan

For the most part, the recommended plan that resulted from this analysis is a composite of the strong points of the various alternatives, and in general it provides significant service improvements in many parts of the service area, primarily through streamlining the existing route network and utilizing resources more efficiently. The new route network consists of eight routes which are throughrouted to form, in effect, four pairs of routes. Through-routing was used as the primary basis for the network design because the rider-interview survey showed that many passengers were making cross-town trips, in particular going from zones in the western portion of the service area to those in the eastern portion, and vice versa. Because the Williamsport area is predominantly a linear city from East to West, and because a substantial proportion of all trips are to or from the CBD, connecting pairs of routes at the CBD was a good way of affording more direct transportation and reducing the need for transferring between buses.

Comparison statistics for the existing system and the newly recommended system are shown in table 6-2. While the recommended system represents a consolidation from ten to eight routes, the total number of route miles is decreased by less than one tenth of one percent, and the total area served by the system is actually increased. Increases in the ratio of route miles to allowed running time result in greater schedule speeds. The total output of the system is, moreover, expanded substantially, with an increase of 18.6 percent in the number of round trips made per day and a 22.7 percent increase in the total number of vehicle miles operated per day. In contrast, the number of vehicle hours operated per day decreased very slightly.

Table 6-2
Comparative Route Characteristics, Existing and Recommended Systems

Route Name	Route Miles	Weekday Trips	Vehicle Miles per Day	Running Time (minutes)	Schedule Speed (mph)	Vehicle Hours per Day
Existing System						
Newberry	6.6	31	204.6	30	13.2	15.5
Montoursville	13.8	31	427.8	60	13.8	31.0
Campbell St.	3.4	25	85.0	30	6.8	12.5
4th St.	4.7	18	84.6	30	9.4	9.0
South Side	7.8	29	226.2	30	15.6	14.5
East End	4.4	29	127.6	30	8.8	14.5
Penn Vale	10.3	17	175.1	45	13.7	12.8
Garden View	10.3	22	226.6	60	10.3	22.0
Park Avenue	4.2	12	50.4	30	8.4	6.0
Reach Road	8.0	5	40.0	60	8.0	5.0
Totals	73.5	188	1647.9		11.5	142.8
Recommended Plan Route Statistics						
4th St.-						
Newberry	11.1	29	321.9	45	14.8	21.75
Montoursville	13.8	29	400.2	45	18.4	21.75
East End	7.0	29	203.0	30	14.0	14.5
South Side	8.0	28	224.0	30	16.0	14.0
Park Ave.-						
Garden View	9.1	28	254.8	45	12.1	21.0
Loyalsock	9.2	26	239.2	45	12.3	19.45
3rd St.-						
Reach Road	11.1	25	277.5	40	16.6	16.71
N. Market St.	3.5	29	101.5	20	10.5	9.67
Totals	72.8	223	2022.1		14.6	138.83

While vehicle miles per day is the major output measure of the system, vehicle hours (which could also be viewed as an output measure) serves as an indirect indication of operating costs, since many cost items, especially drivers' wages, vary directly with vehicle hours. Thus, in providing for a substantial increase in vehicle miles per day while retaining roughly the same number of vehicle hours, the new system is a marked improvement in terms of internal operating efficiency. This is further reflected by the fact that vehicle miles per hour, or average schedule speed, operated by the buses increased from 11.5 to 14.6 with the new plan, an indication of more efficient vehicle utilization.

Program Logic and Implementation

While the major emphasis of the original study was on improving the overall service plan, it was understood that other components of the Williamsport Bureau of Transportation's program would have to be improved if a substantial increase in ridership were to be achieved. Figure 6-1 shows the underlying logic of the transit-improvement program. This systems diagram looks somewhat different from the others in this book, primarily because the "program" of interest here is an improved version of a previously existing public service. Thus the elements reflect the implementation of recommendations for service changes, and outputs are not shown in the figure because, for the most part, they would be redundant statements indicating the extent to which output levels changed.

The improvements in the operations component, as described earlier, were intended to lead to reduced travel times, reduced walking distances between bus stops and origins and destinations, and fewer and more convenient transfers. However, these linking variables were thought to be necessary, but *not* sufficient, conditions for generating additional ridership.

Parenthetically, it should be noted that ridership on transit systems is often taken as a self-evident indicator of the usefulness of public transportation and the appropriateness of heavily subsidizing such systems. As indicated in figure 6-1, support for transit systems is often justified further in terms of subsequent impacts which are anticipated as spinoffs from improvements in service levels designed in great part to attract more ridership. These include increased mobility—particularly for those who do not have private transportation available—and increased downtown business, as well as decreased downtown traffic congestion, improved parking in the CBD, and increased fuel efficiency. However, these last three categories are most salient in the nation's largest metropolitan areas and are less apt to materialize in smaller urban areas. In smaller cities such as Williamsport, improved public transportation may well have some impact on overall mo-

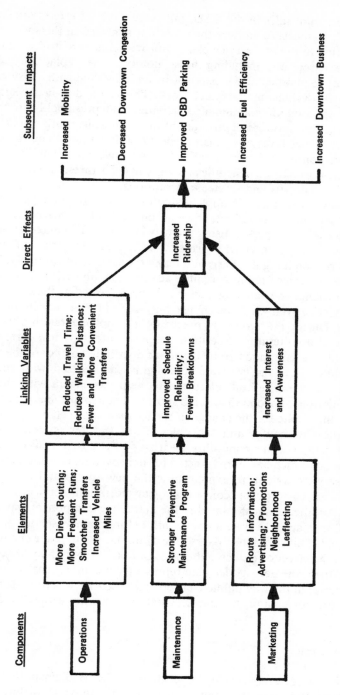

Figure 6-1. Williamsport Transit-Improvement Program.

bility and on retail sales in the CBD, but these kinds of effects are elusive and difficult to measure and are therefore not analyzed in this evaluation.

In addition to the new service plan, improvements were instituted in the maintenance program, including most notably, the replacement of a nonmechanic as maintenance supervisor by an individual with considerable familiarity with vehicle maintenance work. This resulted in better supervision and inspection of maintenance activities and presumably in better-quality work. Furthermore, a program of more rigorous routine preventive maintenance procedures was instituted. Overall, these changes in the maintenance component were intended to improve the reliability of the system as measured by on-schedule arrivals and departures, and the number of vehicle breakdowns and service interruptions.

It was also clear that the implementation of a whole new plan of bus routes and schedules would have to be accompanied by a marketing effort geared to assist passengers in using the new system and to make its advantages known to potential new riders. The great majority of transit passengers ride on a regular basis and make the same trips routinely. Thus, any change in service plan may require adjustments on their part, and furthermore a change in route alignments may be perceived as the elimination of certain service even when the change may afford better service for a particular trip. During the two weeks preceding the implementation of the new service, therefore, literature describing the new routes and how various trip needs would be accommodated by them was distributed on board the buses.

In addition, the drivers were thoroughly familiarized with the new system well in advance and instructed to help passengers with their individual questions. Beyond this, radio spots and newspaper space were used to prepare the public for the change in service plan and spell out the advantages of the new routes and schedules. Once the new system was implemented and working smoothly, leaflets were distributed in various neighborhoods which had been targeted for improved service and new ridership. These were written to explain how the new routes and connections were tailored to provide convenient transportation service to those residents. Another element related to the marketing component was the initiation of an exact-fare system one month before the new service plan was implemented. This saved the drivers time by not having to make change, but it also had the effect of reducing the price of tokens from 25 to 20 cents. In summary, then, the new service plan represented a comprehensive and very distinct change in the way public-transportation service was provided in the Williamsport area, and its implementation was immediate and very thorough.

Evaluation Design

In choosing a research design for evaluating the Williamsport Transit-Improvement Program, the analysts faced a situation which differed from the other two case studies presented in this book in that the program to be evaluated was implemented on an areawide basis as opposed to being targeted in discrete areas. Thus a comparative program/no-program design on the basis of blocks or neighborhoods was out of the question. For this reason, the impacts produced by changes in transit-system operations are generally evaluated on a longitudinal basis. Many studies, for example, have used the immediate before-and-after comparison approach,[7] while fewer evaluations have been based on the extended time-series approach.[8] In general, the evaluations of transit service improvements and the effects of fare changes using such longitudinal approaches have yielded mixed results, and there is still much to learn in this area.[9]

Since fairly reliable data on the transit system's performance on a monthly basis were available from 1975 until the time when the evaluation was conducted, it was decided to use an extended time-series approach. This allowed for consideration of experience with the new system for one full year after implementation. The basic design of this evaluation, then, is a single-time-series design with measures taken on the entire system for each given month. A single-time-series, as opposed to multiple-time-series, design is appropriate here because preprogram trends were clearly deteriorating and there were no environmental shifts occurring simultaneously which could be reasonably thought to confound the impacts of the transit-improvement program.

One interesting aspect of this evaluation is that a wide variety of indicators are observed on this monthly time-series basis, all relating to the program logic displayed in figure 6-1.[10] First, trends in the number of vehicle miles operated per day are examined as the principal measure of the transit system's output. Second, two indicators of service quality are analyzed over time as linking variables intended to induce greater usage of the system. The number of vehicle breakdowns, including service interruptions as well as more minor breakdowns, are viewed as an approach to evaluating the performance of the maintenance component. The effect of the more direct routing is assessed in part by looking at the number of transfers required to make trips; since total trip making was expected to increase with the implementation of the new system, transfers are analyzed in terms of the ratio of transfers to the total number of passenger trips.

The direct effects of the new system are evaluated by analyzing trends in total ridership before and after the new routes were implemented. The primary indicator here is the total number of passengers (or total number of one-way passenger trips) per day. It should be noted, however, that the system's ridership includes senior citizens who ride the bus for free during off-peak hours from 9 a.m. until 3:30 p.m. along with the regular fare-paying passengers. In order to separate the effects on these two groups, another indicator, the percent revenue passengers, is also analyzed. Ridership is also related to the major output measure through the use of two additional variables, passengers per vehicle mile and revenue passengers per vehicle mile, in order to determine whether the increase in vehicle mileage had a disproportional effect on additional ridership.

The next set of variables analyzed pertain to the cost of operating the system. The Williamsport Bureau of Transportation's total expense per month is analyzed since January 1975 to assess the bureau's success in holding the line on costs while increasing service provision. This cost is also related to output with the cost per vehicle mile variable as an indicator of internal operating efficiency. Moreover, cost is related to ridership by examining trends in the cost per passenger variable in order to evaluate the cost-effectiveness of the new system.

The final indicators analyzed across the extended time period pertain to revenue and financial performance. Total revenue per day is examined in order to evaluate the impact of increasing ridership on earned revenues; this would be expected to increase, particularly if the additional ridership tended to consist disproportionally of revenue passengers as opposed to free-fare senior citizens. Finally, the percent cost recovery variable, the ratio of total revenue to total costs, is examined over time to determine the impact of the new system on the Williamsport Bureau of Transportation's deficit and needs for subsidy.

A complementary aspect of the evaluation was a comparison of data obtained in the original onboard rider interview survey discussed earlier with similar data collected in the same kind of survey seventeen months later, well after the new system had been put into effect. This before-and-after comparison expands the scope of the evaluation somewhat by permitting passenger evaluations to be taken into account.

Notes

1. See American Public Transit Association, *Transit Fact Book 1976-77* or *1977-78* (Washington: American Public Transit Association), for a presentation of national trends in urban mass transit over the past 35 years.

2. Herman Mertins, Jr., and David R. Miller, "Urban Transportation Policy: Fact or Fiction?" *Urban Transportation Policy: New Perspectives* (Lexington, Mass.: Lexington Books, 1972).

3. George W. Hilton, *Federal Transit Subsidies* (Washington: American Enterprise Institute for Public Policy Research, 1974); and George M. Smerk, *Urban Mass Transportation: A Dozen Years of Federal Policy* (Bloomington: Indiana University Press, 1974).

4. A complete description of this original study and its findings and recommendations can be found in Theodore H. Poister, *1977 Transit Update: Williamsport Area Transportation Study* (Harrisburg: Pennsylvania Department of Transportation, 1978).

5. See Urban Transportation Systems Associates, Inc., *Urban Mass Transportation Travel Surveys* (Washington: U.S. Department of Transportation, 1972), for a description of alternative methods for surveying patterns of transit usage.

6. See Herbert S. Levinson, *Bus Transit Service Planning Guide*, TRB Synthesis Report No. 7-09 (*forthcoming*, 1979), for a review of the state of the art of the design of routes and schedules for bus transit systems. See also, John Dickey, *Metropolitan Transportation Planning* (Washington: Scripta, 1975).

7. Roosevelt Steptoe and Theodore Poister, "Mass Transportation Demands of Scotlandville Residents," *Highway Research Record*, No. 419 (1972), pp. 16-26; Kenneth J. Dueker and James Stoner, "Examination of Improved Transit Service," *Highway Research Record*, No. 419 (1972), pp. 27-36; George M. Smerk, "Experiments in Urban Transportation," *Business Horizons* (Summer 1964), pp. 39-47.

8. Michael A. Kemp, *Transit Improvements in Atlanta—The Effects of Fare and Service Changes* (Washington: Urban Institute, 1974).

9. Michael A. Kemp, *The Consequences of Short-Range Transit Improvements: An Overview of a Research Program* (Washington: U.S. Department of Transportation, 1978); Michael A. Kemp and Melvyn D. Cheslow, "Transportation," in *The Urban Predicament*, William Gorham and Nathan Glazer, (eds.) (Washington: Urban Institute, 1976), pp. 281-356.

10. See Dennis F. McCrosson, "Choosing Performance Indicators for Small Transit Systems," *Transportation Engineering*, March 1978, pp. 26-30; Gordon J. Fielding, Roy E. Glauthier and Charles A. Lave, "Applying Performance Indicators in Transit Management," *Proceedings of the First National Conference on Transit Performance* (Washington: U.S. Department of Transportation, 1977), for discussions of indicators of transit system performance.

7

Impact Assessment and Plan Modification

The followup study in Williamsport, conducted a year after the new transit plan was implemented, was designed both to evaluate the effectiveness of the new system and to determine whether further adjustments in the service plan were needed. This chapter is concerned primarily with the analysis of changes in outputs, linking variables, and direct effects using the extended time-series approach and simple before-and-after comparisons. In addition, some analysis of current operations under the new system is presented to provide an idea of the formative nature of the followup evaluation in terms of developing recommendations for modifications in the service plan.

Time-Series Analysis

The principal method of assessing the impact of the new system in this evaluation is to analyze extended time series before and after the new service plan was put into effect. The indicators representing outputs, linking variables, and effects are observed on a monthly basis from January 1975 through September 1978. Since the new system was implemented in September 1977, this provides for two years and nine months of pre-implementation data and one complete year of postimplementation data. In effect, the pre-implementation time series is analyzed to determine what trend, if any, is apparent in the data leading up to the point when the new system was put into operation. The postimplementation series is then examined to see whether it represents a continuation of what was happening in the pre-implementation series or whether it looks like a significant change from trends before implementation of the new system.

The transit-improvement program's objectives and underlying logic specify the directions in which the various indicators should move after the program was implemented. In general, then, if the postimplementation series differ from trends in the pre-implementation series in the directions predicted by the program logic, it is concluded that the improvement program did have the desired kind of effect.

The most straightforward way of analyzing time-series data is the visual inspection of the data in graphical form. Graphs called *scattergrams* are constructed with the time periods observed, in this case months, along the horizontal axis and the indicators to be analyzed on the vertical axis. Over each time period in the series a dot is located to show the level of the given indicator for that particular period or observation. It is also helpful to draw in a vertical line indicating the time when the new program or policy intervention was implemented. Connecting the dots with a line will provide a clearer visual impression of month-to-month fluctuations and whether any longer-term trend is apparent. To help further in clarifying longer-term trends, it is often useful to draw in straight lines or curves which summarize the visual impression of the pattern of variation across time. The comparison of these *predominant-trend lines* for the pre-intervention and postintervention series is at the heart of the analysis of the program's impact.

Before looking at the results of this analysis, two technical points regarding time-series analysis should be noted. First, the data shown in most of the scattergrams which follow have been *deseasonalized*, or adjusted to extract the month-to-month fluctuations in the data which are due to regular seasonal variation. This was necessary because transit ridership varies systematically on a seasonal basis, tending, for example, to be extraordinarily high in December (for holiday shopping) and low in the summer months. This deseasonalization was accomplished by dividing each raw value by an index score which reflects the extent to which that particular month was greater or less than the mean average for the year. Second, the predominant-trend lines shown in the scattergrams were not drawn in freehand, as might have been done, particularly where the trends are obvious. Instead, a statistical technique known as *regression analysis* was used to arrive at straight lines which best summarize the pre-implementation and postimplementation trends. (See appendix A for a brief discussion of the use of regression analysis as applied to time-series data, along with an example of deseasonalizing time-series data.)

The Internal Operation

The new service plan provided for many more vehicle miles of operation per day. Although this primary measure of output of the transit system increased, vehicle hours are about the same with the new service plan as with the previous service plan. The dramatic increase in vehicle miles per day is shown in figure 7-1. There is an increase of 300 or so vehicle miles per day after September 1977, when the new service plan was put into effect. The remaining variation around the predominant-trend lines is relatively minor and represents seasonal adjustments (these data are *not* deseasonalized) plus variation in the amount of charter service provided each month.

A major indicator of internal operating efficiency is the cost per vehicle mile. As shown in figure 7-2, the cost per vehicle mile was increasing at a

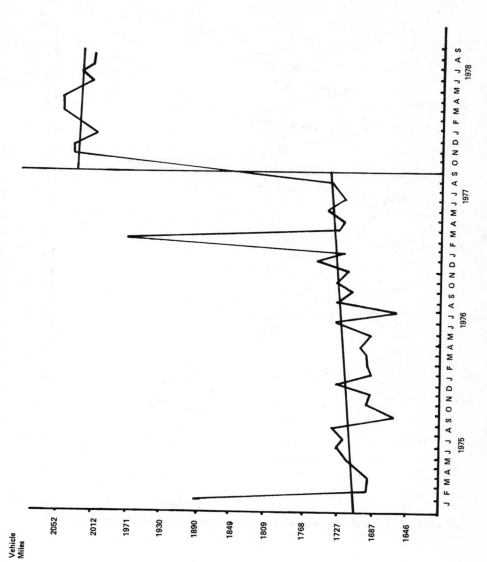

Figure 7-1. Vehicle Miles per Day (Unadjusted).

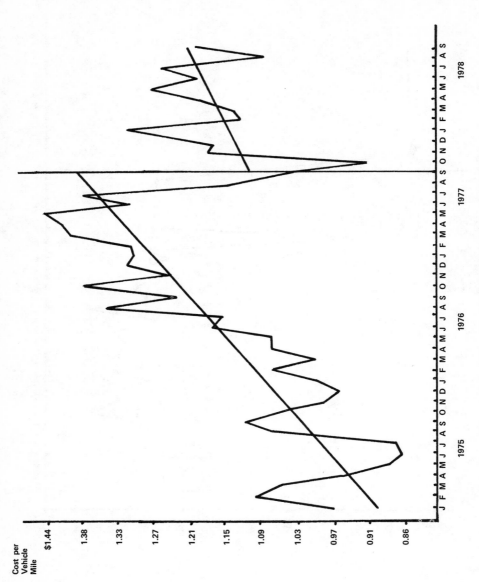

Figure 7-2. Cost per Vehicle Mile (Deseasonalized).

steady rate, then fell dramatically when the new system was put into effect. Since then this indicator has tended to increase at a somewhat lesser rate. What this means is that costs were not increased by virtue of increasing the level of service provided. Operating more vehicle miles per day did not in itself raise the cost of operating the system. Therefore, as the number of vehicle miles was increased with the new system, the cost per vehicle mile went down. Its tendency to increase since that time shows a continuation of the increase in cost due to inflation.

Unfortunately, reliable data on the number of vehicle breakdowns are not available because of changes in the way that this information was recorded and the general sloppiness of record-keeping in the maintenance department before 1977. This makes it difficult to obtain an accurate quantified indication of the extent to which the improved preventive-maintenance program has been effective in reducing the number of inservice breakdowns. However, the vehicle records which log in all maintenance activity do show that substantially more effort is going into preventive activities while less time and effort are going into repairs and unscheduled maintenance work. This would tend to corroborate the general impression of individuals associated with the transit system that the rate of vehicle breakdowns, and particularly real service interruptions, has been reduced.

Linking Variables

One of the ways the new system of routes and schedules was expected to improve service to regular passengers and help to attract additional riders was to reduce walking distances between their homes and the nearest bus stops and between bus stops and their destinations. Table 7-1 shows the distribu-

Table 7-1
Walking Distances with Old and New Systems

Blocks Walked	1976 Survey	1978 Survey
To Bus Stop:		
1 or less	56.6%	68.6%
2	24.2%	17.0%
3	10.5%	7.6%
4	4.8%	2.9%
5 or more	3.9%	4.1%
To Destination:		
1 or less	57.7%	67.1%
2	25.3%	18.0%
3	9.5%	7.6%
4	4.1%	2.9%
5 or more	3.4%	4.4%

tions of distances walked to and from bus stops by passengers responding to the rider surveys taken before and after the new system was implemented. It shows that for distances walked to the bus stop and from the bus stop to the destination, there has been a healthy increase in the percentage of passengers who said that they had to walk only one block or less. This one-block cutoff point is important given the high percentage of elderly people who use the transit system and the inclement weather conditions which prevail much of the year. Conversely, smaller proportions of riders are now walking two or three blocks, while roughly the same proportions walk four, five, or more blocks.

Further analysis of these data showed that these distributions for the 1978 survey responses, after the new system was in use, were virtually identical for new riders and continuing riders. Thus the new system did serve to reduce walking distances in the aggregate for those riders who had been using the system with the old routes and schedules, and it also made the system more attractive in terms of required walking distances for those who became new riders since the new system was put into effect.

A second linking variable which would have been useful in analyzing the extent to which service improved is the average time passengers spend waiting for the bus. Unfortunately, such data were not collected as part of the evaluation. If the before-and-after comparative evaluation had been in mind when the original study was being designed, questions on waiting time could have been included in the two rider surveys.

Data on a third linking variable, transfers from one route to another, are shown in figure 7-3. The through-routing pattern was intended to reduce the need for transfers, and thus the proportion of trips requiring a transfer would be expected to decrease. As shown in figure 7-3, the proportion of transfers after September 1977 is generally lower than before that time, but this comparison is inconclusive because the trend was falling in the preprogram series and increasing in the postprogram series. There is considerable month-to-month fluctuation in the series, and seasonal variation may be unduly influencing these trends. If data on transfers had been available for a longer preprogram series, this analysis might have been more meaningful.

Program Impacts

Changes in ridership are shown in figures 7-4 and 7-5. Figure 7-4 shows total passengers per day, which was declining gradually from January 1975 through August 1977 and then began to increase at a steep rate after the new system was put into effect. This change in the trend of total passengers per day is probably the most important indicator of the *effectiveness* of the new

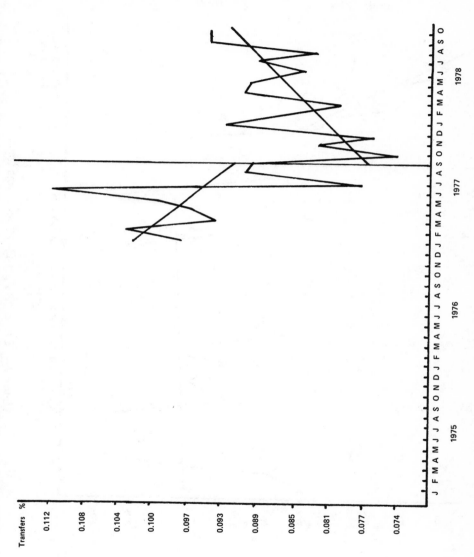

Figure 7-3. Percent Transfers, January 1977 to October 1978 (Unadjusted).

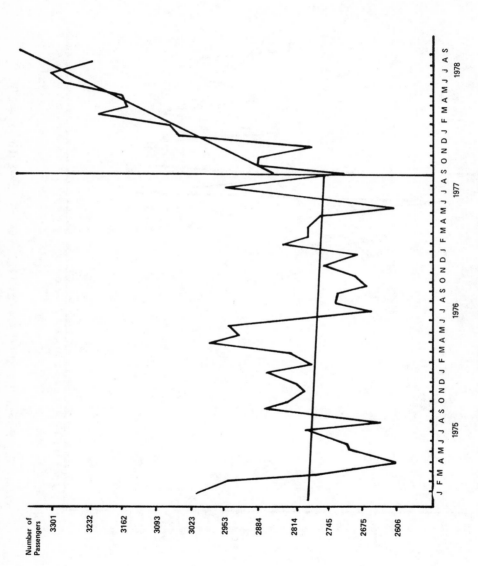

Figure 7-4. Passengers per Day (Deseasonalized).

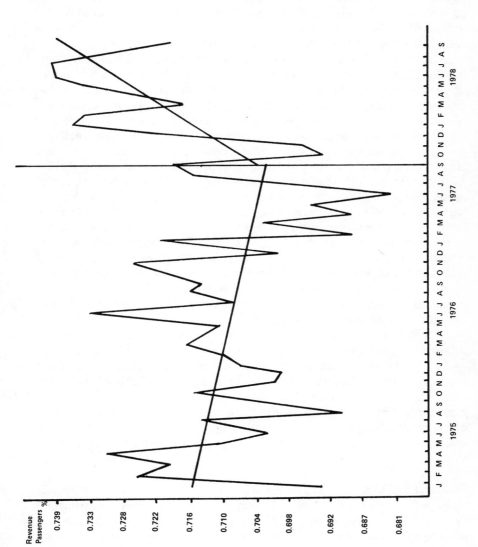

Figure 7-5. Percent Revenue Passengers (Deseasonalized).

system. Furthermore, this increase in ridership has come more from an increase in revenue passengers than from an increase in senior citizens who ride the bus for free between the hours 9 a.m. and 3:30 p.m. As shown in figure 7-5, the percent revenue passengers follows a pattern similar to total passengers. The percentage of total passengers who were revenue passengers was declining in the pre-implementation series and then began to increase substantially in the postimplementation series.

Conversely, the percent senior citizens (not shown) was increasing during the period from January 1975 through August 1977 and then began to decrease sharply after the new system was put into effect. In actuality, the absolute number of senior citizens using the transit system, aside from seasonal variation, has remained pretty much static since the free-fare senior citizen plan was put into effect. As revenue passengers declined, the percentage of senior citizens therefore increased. This trend was reversed finally when the new service plan was put into effect in September 1977.

One measure of the *efficiency* of the transit system is the number of passengers per vehicle mile, shown in figure 7-6. This indicator was decreasing gradually across the pre-implementation series, where vehicle miles operated were pretty much static. Right after September 1977, the number of passengers per vehicle mile dropped substantially, since vehicle miles increased dramatically while total ridership was about the same. Since total ridership has picked up substantially from the time the new system was implemented, however, the average number of passengers per vehicle mile has increased steadily. The number of revenue passengers per vehicle mile (not shown) has followed the same pattern.

As can be seen in figure 7-7, the cost per passenger carried by the system followed a pattern somewhat similar to that of cost per vehicle mile. Prior to the new system, the cost per passenger was increasing steadily, since costs were increasing and total passengers were decreasing. After September, the cost per passenger decreased, since costs remained constant while passengers increased. Since that time, the cost per passenger has tended to decrease slightly. Since costs are continuing to increase, this lower level of cost per passenger can be maintained only by continuing growth in ridership.

Financial Performance. Figure 7-8 shows that revenue per day, which was falling off before the new system was implemented, has been increasing at a fast rate since September 1977, along with the increase of revenue passengers. Figure 7-9 shows that total expense has also been increasing since the new system was implemented. Total expense was increasing at a steady rate before the new system was put into effect and then decreased substantially, and since then has continued to increase at about the same rate.

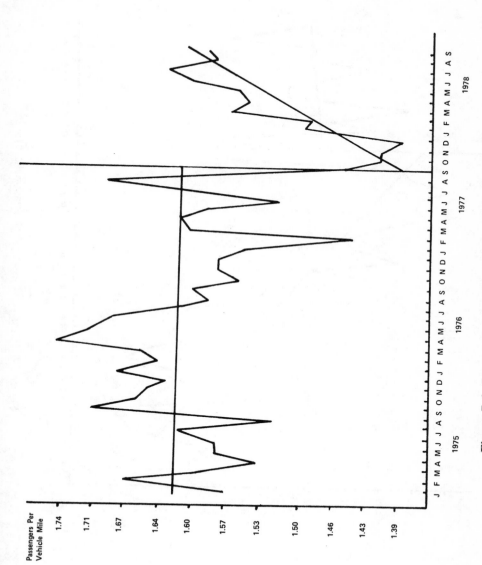

Figure 7-6. Passengers per Vehicle Mile (Deseasonalized).

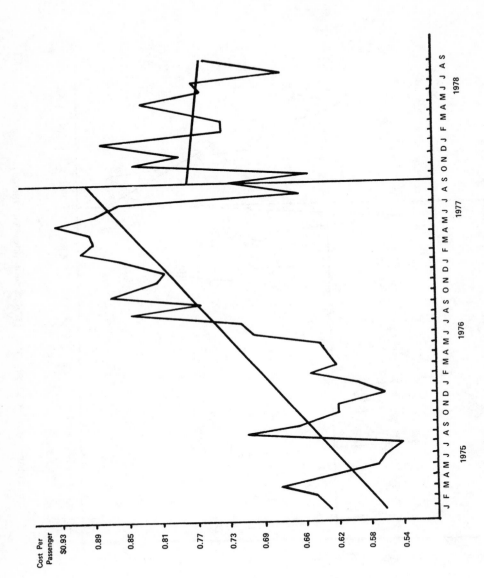

Figure 7-7. Cost per Passenger (Deseasonalized).

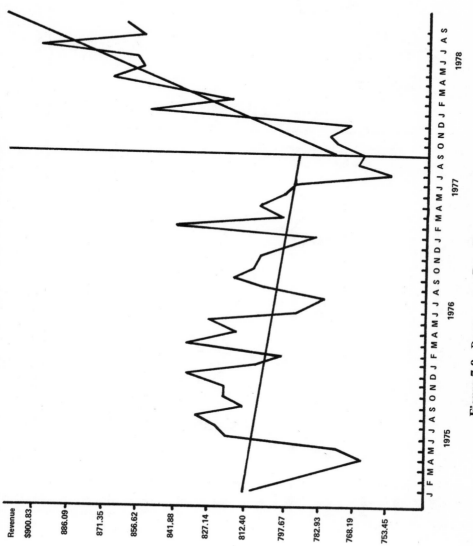

Figure 7-8. Revenue per Day (Deseasonalized).

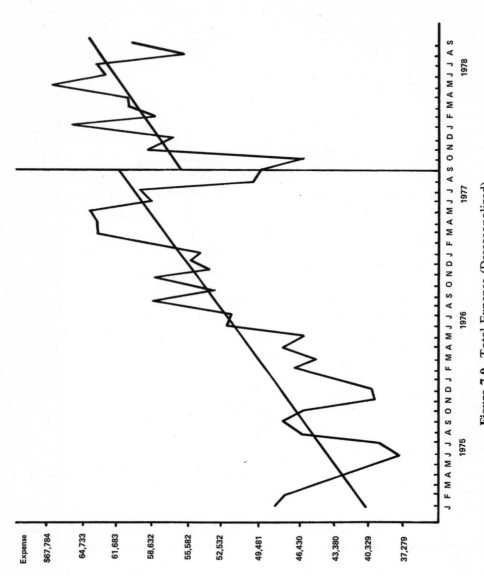

Figure 7-9. Total Expense (Deseasonalized).

In terms of financial efficiency, a major concern of the transit management and city hall is the extent to which the transit operation pays for itself or the extent to which it must be subsidized. Figure 7-10 shows the average deficit incurred by the system per day. This deficit was increasing steadily in the pre-implementation series, then dropped substantially and since September 1977 has been increasing at about the same rate as in the pre-implementation series. Figure 7-11 shows an indicator of the financial performance, percent cost recovery. The percentage of total costs recovered through the fare box and through the senior citizen funds received from the state was decreasing steadily across the pre-implementation series, ranging from roughly 50 percent down to 31 percent. With the new system the percent cost recovery increased by 4 percent or more but has decreased since then. What these last two figures show, therefore, is that the new system has impacted on the level of financial efficiency of the system but not on the rate of change in the financial picture of that system. The deficit per day incurred by the system continues to go up and the percent cost recovery in the system continues to go down. This is almost totally a function of a continuing cost increase due to inflation. The new system did, however, provide some relief to this decaying financial picture by attracting more revenue passengers and therefore increasing revenue over time.

Comparative Ratings

Another way to assess the effectiveness of a service-improvement program is to compare passenger evaluations of the transit system before and after the new system was put into effect. Table 7-2 shows passenger ratings of various aspects of the service in the 1976 and 1978 surveys. In general the pattern of responses obtained in both surveys is quite similar. The only marked differences of a positive nature are that a greater percentage of the respondents in the 1978 survey rated bus frequency as being very good or good, and a greater percentage of respondents in the 1978 survey also rated the fare structure as being either good or very good. These two differences are quite obviously due to the initiation of the exact-fare system and the fact that the new set of schedules provides for half-hour headways on all routes. The only significant difference of a negative nature is that more respondents in the 1978 survey than in the 1976 survey rated the condition of the buses as being only fair or poor. As indicated earlier, the Williamsport Bureau of Transportation is interested in acquiring new buses, but in the meantime, while its maintenance efforts are somewhat improved, the overall condition of the bus fleet continues to deteriorate.

Respondents to the 1978 survey, like those in the 1976 survey, were asked to indicate which, if any, of several possible improvements they thought

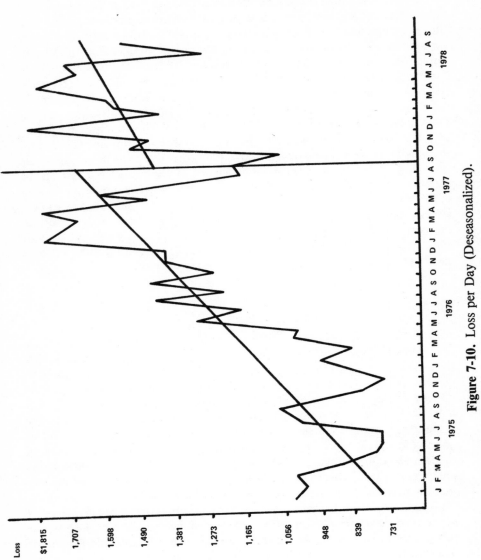

Figure 7-10. Loss per Day (Deseasonalized).

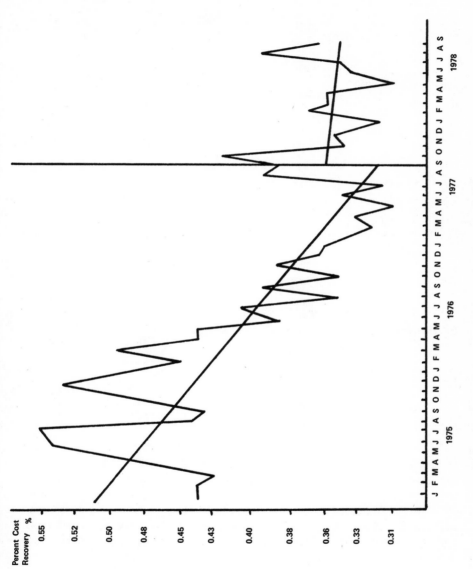

Figure 7-11. Percent Cost Recovery (Deseasonalized).

Table 7-2
Comparative Passenger Ratings

Category	Ratings	1976 (%)	1978 (%)	Percent Change
Route coverage	Very good	24.0	32.0	+8.0
	Good	52.0	44.5	−7.5
	Fair	16.0	18.9	+2.9
	Poor	8.0	4.6	−3.4
Convenience of transfers	Very good	32.0	37.0	+5.0
	Good	56.0	49.2	−6.8
	Fair	10.0	10.5	+0.5
	Poor	2.0	3.3	+1.3
Bus frequency	Very good	20.0	28.0	+8.0
	Good	53.0	51.1	−1.9
	Fair	23.0	18.4	−4.6
	Poor	4.0	2.5	−1.5
Schedule reliability	Very good	22.0	25.9	+3.9
	Good	48.0	47.4	−0.6
	Fair	22.0	22.0	0
	Poor	8.0	4.7	−3.3
Condition of buses	Very good	13.0	11.7	−1.3
	Good	46.0	37.5	−8.5
	Fair	30.0	35.2	+5.2
	Poor	11.0	15.6	+4.6
Driver competence	Very good	42.0	41.4	−0.6
	Good	48.0	47.1	−0.9
	Fair	9.0	9.3	+0.3
	Poor	1.0	2.2	+1.2
Driver courtesy	Very good	49.0	48.3	−0.7
	Good	41.0	39.0	−2.0
	Fair	8.0	9.8	+1.8
	Poor	2.0	2.9	+0.9
Fares	Very good	17.0	29.7	+12.7
	Good	45.0	47.7	+2.7
	Fair	32.0	19.4	−12.6
	Poor	6.0	3.2	−2.8

were necessary or desirable for the Williamsport transit system. The results are shown in table 7-3. There are few interesting differences in the responses to the two surveys. In general, smaller percentages of the respondents to the 1978 survey indicated that various types of improvements were necessary, perhaps indicating in part a general improvement in overall satisfaction with the system. However, the types of improvements which were cited most often were the same for both surveys. These include a desire for benches and bus shelters, for Sunday service, and for more evening service.

Service-Plan Refinements

In addition to assessing the impact of the transit-improvement program on ridership and financial performance, the followup study was concerned

Table 7-3
Needed Improvements

Type of Improvement	Estimated Percent Responding (1976)	Estimated Percent Responding (1978)[a]	Percent Change
Routes closer to destination	8.0	10.5	+2.5
Benches and bus shelters	43.0	30.5	−13.0
New buses	11.0	14.6	+3.6
More rush-hour service	17.0	11.2	−5.8
Better schedule reliability	25.0	16.8	−8.2
Sunday service	40.0	30.1	−9.9
More evening service	36.0	26.2	−9.8
Easier transfers	2.0	1.3	−0.7
Lower steps on buses	8.0	7.9	−0.1
Better route identification	9.0	8.1	−0.9
More frequent off-peak service	−	6.7	−
Better schedule and route information	−	6.1	−

[a]Because respondents could choose several improvements, these percentages will total to greater than 100 percent.

with analyzing the strong and weak points of the new system to determine whether service could be improved further by making adjustments in the plan. For this purpose a number of small (50 to 70 respondents) highly specialized surveys were carried out, and data on operating characteristics, ridership, and costs were collected on an individual route and trip basis for a two-week period. These data bases, along with the systemwide rider survey, permitted a micro-level analysis of the adequacy of various routes and the service provided to certain districts within the service area.

Latent Demand

Home interview surveys were conducted door to door in two particular neighborhoods to determine whether routes should be altered to provide them with more direct service. While similar in nature, these two surveys came about in quite different circumstances. In the first instance, council members from one of the outlying jurisdictions felt that bus service should be operated in a part of the borough which had not had service in the past, primarily because of their desire to provide service on an even basis across the whole jurisdiction. Responses to the survey showed that there was some demand for transit service by residents of the area, and it was recommended that the route in question be modified on every other trip to circulate on those streets before heading for the CBD. The idea was that this should be done for a set period, on a demonstration basis, to note the ridership response and determine whether full service was warranted or not.

The second neighborhood survey was targeted on an area where service had been provided previously but had been withdrawn under the new plan. This service cutback appeared to be the one real mistake in the plan, since the implementation of the new system triggered a stream of complaints about excessive walking distances from that area. This survey revealed a number of residents there who had been regular riders but who stopped using the system when the route was taken away from their neighborhood. Given the substantial proportion of respondents who said they would use the bus if service were restored, including many who had not used it previously, it was recommended that the loop at the end of this particular route be extended in order to serve this area directly.

To get a look at another aspect of the untapped market for transit, a self-administered postcard survey was conducted in Williamsport's largest industrial park. While service was being provided between the CBD and the industrial park, the issue was whether the area should be directly connected with any other area by bus service. Only individuals who were interested in using the bus to get to and from work were intended to be survey respondents. While the total number of respondents was quite small, the data showed that there were quite a few respondents—both regular and potential riders—who lived in two particular residential areas. Both these areas were connected only very indirectly with the industrial park, requiring first a trip to the CBD and then an inconvenient transfer to another bus. This finding led to the development of a new route alignment for the extra commuter bus presently in service that would provide this direct connection without adversely affecting service elsewhere.

Route Analysis

The detailed operating data for the two-week period were analyzed by route and time of day. As an example of the form this analysis took, table 7-4 shows the estimated variable costs (*EVC*) for each route over the two-week period being analyzed. This variable cost was computed by a formula based on the number of vehicle miles and the number of vehicle hours operated for each route, as follows:

$$EVC = \$.28 \text{ (vehicle miles)} + \$6.69 \text{ (vehicle hours)}$$

This estimated variable cost formula was developed by separating out fixed costs from total costs for the month of March and allocating the remaining variable-cost items to either vehicle miles or vehicle hours. The

Table 7-4
Estimated Variable Cost, Revenue, and Operating Loss

Route	Hours	Miles	Estimated Variable Cost[a]	Revenue[b]	Operating Loss	Percent Cost Recovery[c]
1. Newberry	268.17	3,836.80	$2,868	$2,040	$ 853	71.1%
2. Montoursville	275.45	4,957.80	$3,231	$1,524	$1,058	47.2%
3. Gardenview	246.42	3,064.10	$2,506	$1,591	$ 868	63.5%
4. Loyalsock	225.75	3,009.80	$2,353	$1,148	$1,197	50.8%
5. Market Street	113.67	1,248.70	$1,110	$ 418	$ 707	37.6%
6. West Third	192.42	3,149.40	$2,169	$ 936	$1,262	43.1%
7. South Side	174.17	2,422.90	$1,843	$ 814	$ 996	44.2%
8. East End	177.00	2,544.40	$1,896	$ 886	$ 920	46.7%

[a]$EVC = 6.69$ (hours) $+ .28$ (miles).
[b]Includes prorated senior citizen monies.
[c]PCR = revenue $\div EVC$.

total variable cost attributed to vehicle miles was divided by the total number of vehicle miles operated during that month, while the total variable cost attributed to vehicle hours was divided by the total number of vehicle hours during that month. These computations resulted in the two cost coefficients ($.28 and $6.69) shown in the formula.

Table 7-4 shows that the Montoursville route incurred the greatest variable costs, more than $3,000 in the two-week period, followed closely by the Newberry route, which cost close to $3,000 for that period. In the next order of magnitude are the Gardenview route, the Loyalsock route, and the West Third Street route, with total costs ranging from $2,200 to $2,500. These were followed by the South Side and East End routes, which both cost approximately $1,800 to run for the two weeks. Finally the Market Street route cost the least to operate for that two-week period, with an estimated cost of roughly $1,100.

Table 7-4 also shows total revenue, including the senior citizen money received from the state, prorated across the routes according to the number of senior citizens who ride on each route. The distribution of total revenue is quite similar to that of total passengers, with the Newberry route, which has the highest revenue, bringing in roughly five times as much revenue as the Market Street route, which is the route bringing in the least revenue. In terms of total revenue as opposed to direct revenue, the Park Avenue-Gardenview route ranks slightly ahead of the Montoursville route.

The table also shows the estimated operating loss for each route. This operating loss is computed by subtracting total revenue for the route from the total estimated variable cost for the route. As shown in the table, the route which incurred the greatest operating loss is the Montoursville route, with an estimated loss of more than $1,600. Two other routes, the Loyalsock route and the West Third Street route lost more than a thousand dollars each. The Newberry route, the Park Avenue-Gardenview route, the South Side route, and the East End route all lost in the neighborhood of $850 to $1,000 over the two-week period, while the Market Street route had the lowest operating loss, approximately $700. A complementary measure, percent cost recovery, shows that the Market Street route is considerably less cost-effective than the other routes in the system.

In other words, while the Market Street route is the least productive route in terms of the number of passengers carried and the amount of revenue generated, it also cost the least to operate. Nevertheless, taken together these data do indicate that the Market Street route is the sorest spot of the system at present and that there is a greater need for improving performance in that area than in any other sector of the service area.

It was also useful to examine some of the same statistics in terms of time-of-day profiles. Figure 7-12 shows the distribution of variable costs, revenues, and operating loss for the entire system for the two-week period. It shows that revenue increases at an almost steplike fashion across the day until it peaks at the period from 3 p.m. to 4 p.m., then drops off from 4 p.m. to 5 p.m. and again from 5 p.m. to 6 p.m., and then drops off dramatically for the evening hours. Estimated variable costs, on the other hand (shown in figure 7-12), remain constant across the daytime hours from 6 a.m. until 6 p.m., and then are reduced to less than half for the evening hours from 6 p.m. until 10 p.m.

Estimated operating loss, then, fluctuates much more than does revenue or estimated variable costs, as shown in figure 7-12. The greatest operating loss is incurred in the period from 6 a.m. to 7 a.m., when the system is operating at full capacity but is not yet carrying very many passengers. It is estimated that over $800 is lost by operating during that hour across the two-week period being examined. The next highest operating loss was incurred during the period from 5 p.m. to 6 p.m., a period when costs are still high because the system is operating at full capacity while ridership has begun to drop off substantially. From 7 a.m. until 3 p.m., operating loss drops off almost in step-like fashion, the reverse of the increasing revenue across that time. The least operating cost occurs during the hour from 3 p.m. to 4 p.m.

Finally, it should be noted that while the system is operating at roughly half capacity during the evening hours, because ridership is so low, the loss incurred during the hours from 6 p.m. to 10 p.m. is in the neighborhood of $350 to $450 per hour—roughly equivalent to the operating loss incurred from 1 p.m. to 2 p.m. and 2 p.m. to 3 p.m. The percent recovery factors for these evening hours would be much lower than for any daytime hours. The effect of the low passenger loadings in the evening hours is illustrated for

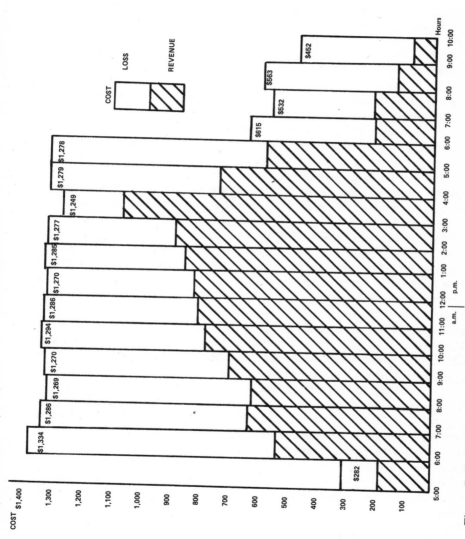

Figure 7-12. Estimated Variable Cost, Revenue, and Operating Loss per Hour Intervals (March 20 to April 1, 1978).

two routes which operate after 6 p.m. in figure 7-13. Estimated deficit per passenger carried, the average amount of subsidy per passenger trip, is much higher on the evening runs than on daytime runs. This raises the issue of whether evening service should be reduced or eliminated, as in most other transit systems in the state. Concerning this point it should be noted that the elimination of service after 6 p.m. would probably result in a net savings of over $3,000 per month to the Williamsport Bureau of Transportation.

Conclusions

The transit-improvement program case study illustrates formative evaluation in the true sense of the word. Using the single-time-series approach, the evaluation demonstrated that the implementation of the new service plan did produce the desired impact of generating increased ridership and improving the system's ratio of revenues to costs. Significant changes in these trends did occur, and there can be little doubt that the program was responsible for them. The evaluation was also able to trace the underlying logic of the program and include most of the relevant outputs and linking variables in the analysis.

Beyond the assessment of program impact, the evaluation was concerned with refinements in the service plan which might be advantageous. This portion of the analysis projected several recommendations for small-scale changes in route configurations which could be put into operation without changing the basic overall service plan. These route changes have to do with modifying or expanding services in the two neighborhoods which were targeted for special surveys, as well as a new alignment for the Market Street route. Another recommendation had to do with a routing and scheduling change which would provide more direct service to the large industrial park which was also surveyed.

In addition, downtown operations were smoothed out on a couple of routes to provide adequate time for the buses to operate on their half-hour schedules, and it was recommended that, given the extremely low ridership on the evening runs, serious consideration be given to eliminating service in the evening after 6 p.m. Taken together, these recommendations represent a set of service changes which are keyed to the same objectives and design principles which served as the basis for developing the new service plan in the first place. The changes recommended in the follow-up study are simply refinements of the new service plan which should lead to even more productive use of the system's resources and hopefully to further incremental growth in ridership.

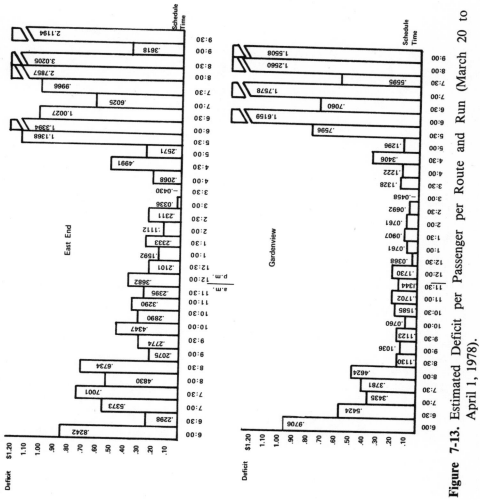

Figure 7-13. Estimated Deficit per Passenger per Route and Run (March 20 to April 1, 1978).

8

The York Crime-Prevention Program Design

Introduction

Crime prevention is often identified as one of the main objectives of law enforcement agencies in this country. Textbooks on municipal police administration usually note the importance of preventing criminality or repressing crime as complementary activities to other police functions: apprehending offenders, recovering property, regulation of noncriminal activities (traffic control, for example), and performance of community services (search and rescue or licensing, for example).[1]

In recent years, crime prevention has grown in importance as police departments and others have recognized the extent to which effective law enforcement involves the community support and cooperation with the police.[2] Crime-prevention programs that emphasize citizen involvement are being implemented as a means of dampening or reversing trends toward higher crime levels. Reduced crime levels in turn are linked by many analysts and police practitioners to improved feelings of safety and security.[3] These benefits in turn are often hypothesized as influences on residents' general attitudes toward their living environments and, more broadly, as influences on their decisions to stay in a particular urban jurisdiction or move elsewhere. The outcome of this latter decision in large part determines the continued viability of larger or older urban communities.

The substance of crime-prevention programs can vary a great deal from one community to another. Local conditions vary, and a well-designed program needs to reflect the nature of the problems facing the police and residents in a given jurisdiction. General strategies can be identified, however. The police themselves can target foot patrol efforts or increase vehicle patrol in areas that are experiencing higher crime rates. Investigative efforts can be targeted on certain types of crimes with the intention of solving a larger proportion and thus demonstrating the consequence of criminal behaviors to potential law breakers, as well as instilling citizen confidence in the police.

Working with citizens, police departments can encourage heightened awareness of security measures that "harden" potential crime targets. Programs in this category would include citizen education and awareness campaigns; efforts to improve the security of homes, businesses, and industrial locations; and property identification and neighborhood watch projects. These programs are intended to multiply the number of "eyes" in a community as a deterrent to crime. Another aspect of this citizen cooperation would include programs geared to encourage improved citizen reporting of crime.

The York Crime-Prevention Program

The city of York, between 1970 and 1974, had experienced substantial increases in levels of reported crimes. By 1974 this trend had been brought to the attention of the mayor, who then appointed a Council on Safe Streets to advise him and the Bureau of Police on strategies to control crime. Specifically, the council was to suggest ways in which crime could be reduced and police effectiveness improved. In the course of its existence, the council has made two major program recommendations:

1. Organization of city blocks into Neighborhood Watch units.
2. Burglary security surveys for residences and businesses in York.

These recommendations were difficult to implement because funds for additional activities were limited. By 1975, continued increases in crime levels and clear expressions of citizen concern suggested the need to mount a concerted effort to prevent crimes. While crime is increasing in all categories at a rate greater than the national average, one of the most serious crimes experienced in York is burglary, both residential and business. The national average for the past five years was 127 burglaries per 10,000 population, with an increase of 47 percent from 1970 to 1974. York experienced 151 burglaries per 10,000 population and an increase of 73 percent over the same period. Since then the rate of increase has been even steeper.

The results of a community survey conducted for the city of York by the Institute of Public Administration at The Pennsylvania State University in the spring of 1976[4] corroborated the perceptions of the police about the seriousness of the crime problem. When asked to respond to a statement that a person is safe from crime in their neighborhood, 246 (49 percent) of the 499 respondents disagreed, while only 161 (32 percent) agreed with the statement. Additional inquiries revealed that 153 (31 percent) of the respondents perceived that crime is increasing, and a slight majority, 252 (51 percent), viewed the crime rate as being stable. However, when queried about burglary rates, a large majority, 332 (67 percent), viewed burglaries as increasing, and only 94 (19 percent) perceived the burglary rate as remaining the same or decreasing.

The survey also covered victimization experiences of city residents from January 1, 1975 to March 1976. From the survey of 499 households, 142, or 28 percent, reported being victimized in the fifteen months preceding the survey administration. Of these 142 households, 33 were victimized more than once for a total of 175 separate incidents. Table 8-1 shows the victim-survey findings.[5] The most prevalent single crime is burglary, accounting for 35 percent of all victimizations of the respondents surveyed.

Program Objectives

The crime-prevention program was funded by a grant from the Governor's Justice Commission in Harrisburg in January 1976. In April 1976, the Bureau of Police began to implement the crime-prevention program, incorporating major recommendations of the Council on Safe Streets. The program, as outlined in the grant application, had six major objectives, four of which were operational objectives and two of which were impact objectives. The operational objectives were

1. Organization of the city's census tracts into Neighborhood Watch units. In some tracts, several organizations would be created.
2. Security surveys of "most" of the city's business establishments (residential surveys would also be provided, but the number was not specified).
3. Organization of citizen-band volunteers into a crime-reporting communication network.

Table 8-1
Types of Crimes of which Respondents Were Victims

	Type	Number of Mentions	Percent of All Crimes
Part I Person Crimes	Aggravated assault	9	5.2%
	Burglary	7	4.0
Total		16	9.2%
Part I Property Crimes	Burglary	61	35.0%
	Personal theft	40	23.0
	Household theft	21	12.0
	Auto theft	7	4.0
Total		129	74.1%
Part II Crimes[a]	Criminal mischief	30	16.7%
Totals		175	100.0%

[a]Part II Crimes in this table includes six cases that were coded as "Other."

4. Education of the general public about crime-prevention techniques through the dissemination of information.

The two impact objectives that were identified were

5. A reduction of burglaries by 5 percent during the first year of the program.
6. A reduction of crime in general (no specific percentage was stated).

Figure 8-1 depicts the crime-prevention program in York as an operating system. Like all systems, the crime-prevention program has to be viewed as one part of a large public safety system. In addition to affecting its environment, this system will be affected by changes in its environment. The interdependencies between the program and its environment mean that although the program process is geared to reducing burglaries and other crimes, environmental factors can affect variables in the program process and modify the intended relationships between program variables and impacts. In addition, environmental variables can affect crime rates directly. Thus measuring changes in crime rates as indicators of program impacts needs to carefully consider the influences of variables other than those in the program in order to establish the unique effects of the program on crime rates.

Program Design

The crime-prevention program as depicted in figure 8-1 has three components: block-level crime-prevention associations known as Neighborhood Watch units, business and household security surveys, and mass-media information dissemination. The Neighborhood Watch component consists of block organizations sponsored by the Bureau of Police for the purpose of "guarding" the neighborhood. These block-level units are loosely grouped into three sector organizations. During the organization meetings, the police give presentations of burglary-prevention techniques and correct ways of reporting crimes. Printed crime-prevention literature is distributed and persons are encouraged to engrave their valuables with an identification number. Home-burglary-security surveys are discussed and residents are encouraged to let the crime-prevention staff survey their homes. Police representatives are present at the first two block meetings to provide this educational information and assist in the block organization and election of block captains. Thereafter, police representatives are present only at the request of block captains, and Neighborhood Watch members are encouraged to take the initiative and continue to hold meetings and look out for the wel-

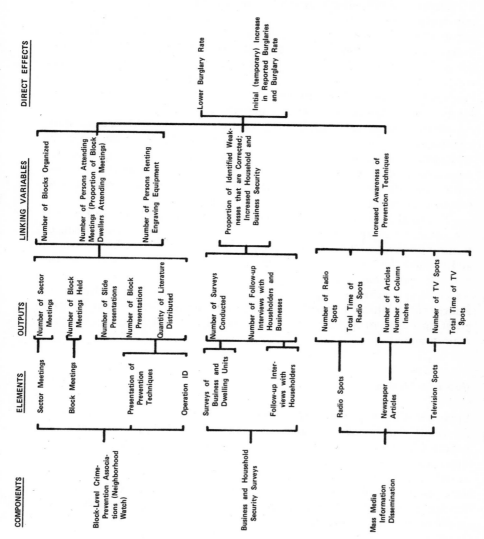

Figure 8-1. York Crime-Prevention Program.

fare of their neighbors as well as to report anything suspicious to the police or the block captain. This component is intended to provide a vehicle for educating citizens, facilitating police-citizen interaction, and site hardening.

Security surveys (the second component) are offered free of charge to any business or residence upon request. Business and dwelling units are surveyed and evaluated according to their burglary security. Weaknesses in locks, doors, windows, lighting, and other burglary-related building features are identified, and the occupants are encouraged to correct these weaknesses. Follow-up surveys are conducted to determine the adequacy of the measures taken. The strategy of this component is that of reducing burglary opportunities through site hardening.

Mass-media dissemination is the third component. York has two daily newspapers and several radio and television stations that can cover the crime-prevention program. Also, special programs and public-service announcements can be aired. The strategy involved is reducing burglary and other crime opportunities through citizen education and the deterrence effect of program publicity.

The final component of the program is not depicted in figure 8-1. It is the volunteer citizen-band emergency reporting network. The Bureau of Police has purchased a CB unit, organized volunteer citizen-band owners, and has assigned them code numbers so that they can directly contact the police to report any crimes or suspicious activities. The underlying strategy is to encourage citizen cooperation and awareness, providing the Bureau of Police with additional "eyes" in the city. During the first year of the program, this component generated comparatively few outputs that were program oriented.

Research Design

In cooperation with the Bureau of Police and the director of public safety, an effort was made to target components of the program into one geographic area of the city while making another area a "control" area. The reasoning behind such a strategy was that comparing the crime trends in the program target area with crime trends in the control area over the time would permit a relatively sound evaluation of the program. Differences in crime trends in the target and comparison areas could be linked to different levels of program activities.

If the program was fully implemented as a comparison time-series quasi-experiment, control areas should not have received any "treatment" (components of the crime-prevention program), whereas the target areas should have received the full impact of the program. However, two of the program components, mass-media information dissemination and the citizen-band emergency reporting network, were intended to include as many city residents as possible, regardless of their geographic location. Thus residents in the control areas as well as those elsewhere in the city were exposed to these components.

Target and Comparison Areas

Another factor which reflects the distributional constraint in implementing the program was the belief that it was unwise to deliberately withhold security surveys or neighborhood block organizations from residents of the nontarget areas of the city. These two components were actively administered in the target areas, but were also provided on a request basis to neighborhoods in the control area and in other parts of the city.

Figure 8-2 depicts the geographic area of York and shows where target areas (census tracts) and control areas were located. The Bureau of Police planner was consulted on the feasibility of grouping different tracts together for the purpose of creating target and control areas. An effort was made to select several contiguous tracts as a program target area and then select a group of tracts that were similar (in general terms) and could serve as a control area. The target area is comprised of census tracts 12, 13, and 14, while the comparison area is comprised of tracts 3, 4, 5, and 6.

Given the size of the city and the heterogeneity among the sixteen census tracts, the program target areas differ somewhat in socioeconomic terms from the control areas. A higher proportion of the population in the target areas is black than in the control area tracts. A higher proportion of the population in the target areas than in the control area tracts has a high school education, and the mean family income for the target areas tends to be higher. The differences that do exist between the control and target areas may reduce their comparability, even though the burglary rates were the same in 1975 (6.8 reported burglaries per 100 households).

The geographic distribution of blocks that were actually organized from the time the program was implemented in April 1976 was much more scattered than an emphasis on the target areas suggests. The Neighborhood Watch component, the key part of the program effort, was implemented not only in the target areas, but in the control areas to some extent. Blocks were also organized in the "nonexperimental" parts of the city. More broadly, the initial research design, with its geographic focus, was eroded by the process of program implementation. Environmental constraints as well as a deliberate citywide effort with respect to the mass-media and citizen-band-reporting components produced program efforts that included all census tracts in the city. This change in implementation strategy became apparent as the program was monitored through its first calendar year (April

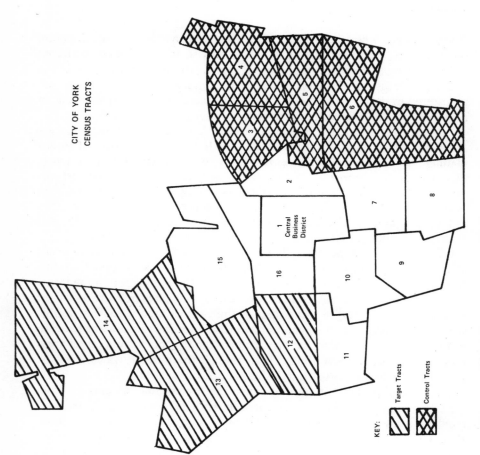

Figure 8-2. City of York Census Tracts.

1976 through March 1977). Improving the efficiency of the research design undergirding the evaluation was clearly a key problem.

The fact that the Neighborhood Watch component was implemented in nearly all census tracts was turned to the advantage of the program evaluators. A decision was made to select a random sample of city blocks that were not organized as Neighborhood Watch units (comparison blocks) and compare the reported crime trends over time in those blocks with trends in the organized (target) blocks. The selection of comparison blocks was done so that there was a comparable number of target and randomly selected comparison blocks for each census tract where any target blocks existed.

Time-Series Approach

The program evaluation was conducted using a comparison time-series research design that focused primarily on city blocks as units of analysis. This level of analysis facilitated examining the effectiveness of the Neighborhood Watch component of the program in particular. As will be seen, this component was by far the most important thrust of the crime-prevention effort in York. Examining the effectiveness of Neighborhood Watch units in reducing crimes (burglaries in particular) offers the fairest test of the hypotheses underlying the program logic displayed in figure 8-1.

The time series used in the evaluation begin in January 1974 (citywide burglary rates) and in January 1975 (comparison and target tracts as well as comparison and target blocks). The main time frame for the evaluation of the program itself is the first full calendar year of its implementation. This coincides with the time frame over which the program was initially funded. Program outputs are aggregated for the first year of operation. Program impact measures are examined on a monthly basis, but because the Neighborhood Watch units that were organized during the first year of the program continued to operate beyond April 1977, the impact indicators are carried through August 1977, the last month before the evaluation report was prepared for the Bureau of Police.

Notes

1. George D. Eastman (ed.), *Municipal Police Administration* (Washington: International City Management Association, 1971), p. 3.

2. Shirley Henke, "A Citizen-Police Partnership in Contra Costa County," *Crime Prevention Review* 5(1), (1977), pp. 25-31; Donald E. Nash, "Crime Prevention through Community Relations," *Crime Prevention Review* 4(1), (1976), pp. 13-19.

3. Jane Jacobs, *The Death and Life of Great American Cities* (New York: Random House, 1961), esp. pp. 29-54; Oscar Newman, *Defensible Space: Crime Prevention through Urban Design* (New York: Macmillan, 1973), esp. pp. 78-101.

4. Theodore H. Poister and James C. McDavid, *A Report of York Residents' Evaluations and Preferences for Local Governmental Programs and Services* (Institute of Public Administration, Pennsylvania State University, 1977).

5. Ibid., p. 283.

Evaluation of the York Crime-Prevention Program

Introduction

Findings of the crime-prevention program evaluation are presented so that outputs of each component are summarized first. Then program impacts are analyzed and discussed. Impact analyses are basically conducted at two levels. At one level, crime trends in the target and control census tracts are examined to see whether program components differentially affected burglaries at this level. Because the mass-media component was intended to affect citywide burglary rates, it is important to briefly examine the pattern of covariation between newspaper coverage of the program and burglary trends for the entire city. At the block level, the evaluation focuses on the effectiveness of the Neighborhood Watch units. By comparing burglary trends in the organized blocks and the comparison blocks it is possible to see whether that program component affected burglary rates.

Following the assessment of program effectiveness, environmental variables that could have influenced burglary rates are discussed. Then conclusions and recommendations are presented. The recommendations for change are intended to guide a reformation of the program to increase its effectiveness.

Program Outputs

Focusing first on the Neighborhood Watch component, outputs during the course of the first program year (April 1976 through March 1977) included 8 sector meetings, 242 block meetings, 75 slide presentations, 192 anticrime block presentations, the distribution of 11,100 pieces of crime literature, including 3,200 pertaining to burglaries, 2,000 pertaining to purse snatching, 2,500 pertaining to rape, and 3,400 property identification lists. In addition, 62 blocks citywide were organized and 247 households rented engraving equipment to mark their valuables. A survey of all block captains (50 out of 62 responded to the survey) yielded an important estimate of participation in block meetings by residents. The average number of adult residents on each block was 41. An average of 10 residents (24 percent) attended block meetings.

Business and household security surveys make up the second component of the program. All told, only twenty-three security surveys were con-ducted, seven of which were conducted for business establishments, the re-mainder for households. No follow-up surveys or interviews were con-ducted by the crime-prevention coordinator to determine if these establishments or households had corrected weaknesses identified by the person conducting the survey. It is worth noting that security surveys were intended to be a key component of the program. The intention of the crime-prevention program planners was to implement security surveys by utilizing personnel from the housing inspection staff of the Department of Com-munity Development. The planned strategy was to combine burglary-security surveys with dwelling-unit codes inspections. Resistance to codes inspections had been a major problem for codes-enforcement staff. Plan-ners of the crime-prevention program hypothesized that free burglary-security surveys would offer an incentive to residents to permit codes in-spections at the same time.

Fire Department personnel were also included as security surveyors. Several joint meetings with housing-inspection and fire personnel were held to explain the security surveys and train personnel to conduct surveys. Time was spent going over the survey instrument itself, as well as showing the security surveyors how to recognize inadequate protection from burglaries in the physical attributes of a dwelling unit or business.

Two types of objections to involving housing or fire personnel in securi-ty surveys surfaced. In the first place, conducting surveys was viewed as ex-tra work by both groups in already crowded schedules. More important, however, some recommended burglary-prevention precautions (locks on windows, bars on windows and doors, for example) were viewed by Fire Department staff as contraventions of fire regulations. Making homes and businesses difficult for burglars to enter also made them difficult for firemen to enter and more difficult for people to exit from in an emergency. It was impossible to reach working compromises, so the housing inspectors and firemen opted out of the crime-prevention program.

Without the active assistance of housing inspectors and firemen, the security-surveys component had to be deemphasized, so surveys were con-ducted only upon request. In fact, very few homes and businesses took ad-vantage of the service during the first program year, indicating that that component was inappropriate given the environment in which the program operated.

The output levels of the third component (mass-media publicity) varied according to the medium. Program evaluators contacted local radio and television stations, and information regarding the number of public-service announcements aired and the duration of these announcements was re-quested. Only one radio station responded to requests for information and stated that no public-service announcements had been broadcasted because the Bureau of Police had never made such a request. The crime-prevention coordinator did tape a one-half-hour radio program and a one-hour television program in which the crime-prevention program was discussed. Each of these programs was aired during April and May of 1977. A total of fifty-five newspaper articles that publicized the program were published during the first program year. The actual space taken by articles was measured by calculating the column-inch equivalent of each article. The distribution of column inches across the first year is displayed in figure 9-2.

The information obtained from the Bureau of Police on the final program component shows that the volunteer citizen-band emergency reporting network had 204 members, and during the first program year, 136 CB calls were received by the Bureau of Police. Members of the network were instructed to call in to report only crimes and emergencies. However, members called in a substantial number of nonemergency occurrences, so that the total number of calls is not an accurate indication of anticrime activity. Also, no records have been kept on police response time or arrest and clearance rates that resulted from responses made to CB calls, making it difficult to accurately measure the impacts (if any) of this program component. Given that the total number of calls for police services in Part I criminal offense situations alone was 6,200 in the twelve-month period from January 1976 through December 1976, the program component in question likely had little effect.

Program Impacts

Figure 9-1 displays burglary trends in the target and control census tracts from January 1974 through August 1977. The vertical line shows when the crime-prevention program was implemented. The preprogram burglary trends (summarized by predominant-trend lines) are similar for both areas of York. They indicate a general *increase* in burglaries moving at a greater rate in the target tracts. The trend lines summarizing both time series during the program period indicate a general *decrease* in burglaries. The rates of decrease for the two areas of the city are quite similar, although the discontinuities in the trend lines for the control census tracts suggest a more substantial drop in burglaries around the time the program was implemented.

The general similarity of the time series for the target and control areas suggests that the manner in which the program was implemented did not produce markedly different trends in these two areas of the city. This finding is consistent with the fact that small proportions of the blocks in the target *and* control areas were organized. Fifteen of the sixty-two organized blocks were located in the three target tracts. This figure represents 13 per-

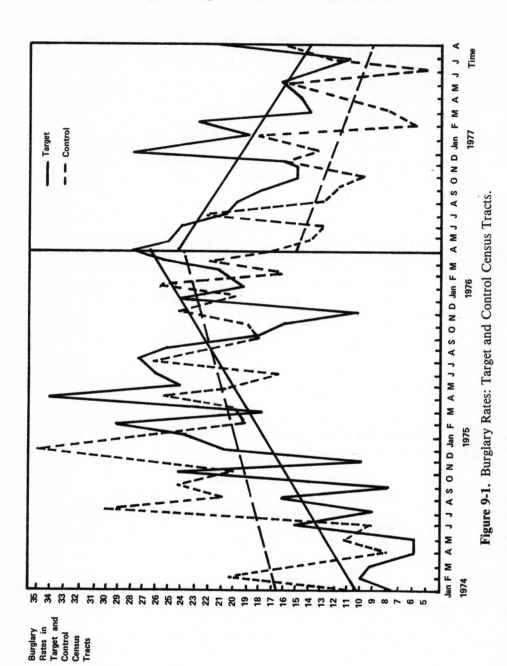

Figure 9-1. Burglary Rates: Target and Control Census Tracts.

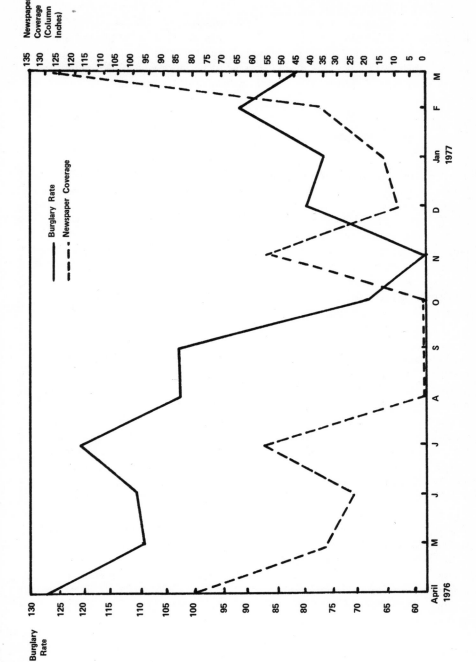

Figure 9-2. Citywide Burglary Rate and Newspaper Coverage (First Program Year).

cent of the 120 blocks existing in those tracts. Five blocks were organized in the four control tracts, representing 4 percent of the 128 blocks in that part of York. Neither percentage is large, suggesting that substantial census-tract-level effects of the Neighborhood Watch component would not likely emerge. Neither percentage would appear to be large enough to constitute the critical mass required to affect tract-level burglary rates.

Citywide Burglary Trends

The citywide burglary trend from January 1974 through August 1977 is generally similar to trends in the target and control areas. Burglaries increased substantially during the two years beginning in January 1974 (1,116 in 1974 and 1,365 in 1975). Figure 9-2 displays the citywide burglary trend through the first program year. The general pattern of decline is compared with the monthly totals of the newspaper coverage of the program (measured in column inches). According to the program logic, media coverage was expected to increase citizens' awareness of crime prevention and prompt them to take preventive measures. This in turn was linked to decreased burglary rates.

The substantial decrease in burglaries in figure 9-2 is not consistently associated with levels of newspaper publicity. During the first several months of the program, publicity and burglary levels covary positively—as publicity increases, so do burglaries. From October through March, the association is generally negative and more consistent with the program logic. Linking newspaper publicity and burglary levels assumes the veracity of several intermediate hypotheses that are not tested in this evaluation. Does newspaper publicity increase citizen awareness of burglary-prevention techniques? Does increased awareness lead to steps intended to make burglaries more difficult? Do these steps lead to a reduction in burglaries? Before increased newspaper coverage is said to "cause" burglary decreases, it is worthwhile to assess the likelihood that the entire sequence is corroborated by evidence. Without direct evidence, the issue is judgmental. When the question of newspaper publicity reducing burglaries was raised with the program planner, he did not believe there was a strong linkage.

Clearly, there is a need to examine other variables that could have influenced citywide burglary rates. Since the mass-media component was the only one implemented that was intended to have a broad impact, it will be important later in the chapter to look at environmental factors that could have affected citywide burglary rates.

Impact of the Neighborhood Watch Units

Organizing the Neighborhood Watch blocks constituted the key set of activities during the first year of the program's operation. Program personnel actively encouraged city residents to form block units and offered considerable assistance in starting such units. The theory behind this component of the program stressed the benefits of citizen-citizen interactions to prevent crime, as well as citizen-police cooperation. Block captains were encouraged to continue holding meetings beyond the startup meetings to keep the block involved in crime prevention. In addition, they were to act as block representatives to the Bureau of Police.

During the first six months of the program, thirty-eight blocks were organized. Thereafter, organizational efforts tapered off. An important reason why program outputs diminished was that a key person in the crime-prevention staff resigned his position as liaison with the block captains during the late fall of 1976. He had been instrumental in organizing new blocks and in motivating block captains to continue crime-prevention efforts beyond the startup meetings. Many block captains expressed keen disappointment to the Bureau of Police at his departure and appeared to be less enthusiastic thereafter.

Data on reported crime levels (burglaries, Part I person, and Part I property) were collected for each of the 124 blocks (62 target and 62 comparison blocks) included in the analysis from January 1975 through August 1977. These data can be used to graph the changes in reported crimes in the target blocks *before* the crime-prevention program was implemented (January 1975 to March 1976) as well as after (April 1976 to August 1977). By comparing that time series to the one generated for the comparison blocks, it is possible to see what effects, if any, the Neighborhood Watch component had on reported crimes over and above environmental influences and citywide program outputs that operated on crime rates.

Figure 9-3 displays the burglary rates for the target and comparison blocks from January 1975 through August 1977. The predominant-trend lines superimposed on both time series indicate a general increase in burglaries through the months prior to any blocks being organized. After the program is initiated, burglaries in the sixty-two target blocks tend to decrease. If this time series were examined alone, it would be reasonable to argue for the effectiveness of the Neighborhood Watch units. But the predominant-trend line in the comparison time series indicates a substantial drop in burglaries on these blocks too. Thus, with *no* Neighborhood Watch units, burglaries nevertheless declined in a set of randomly selected city

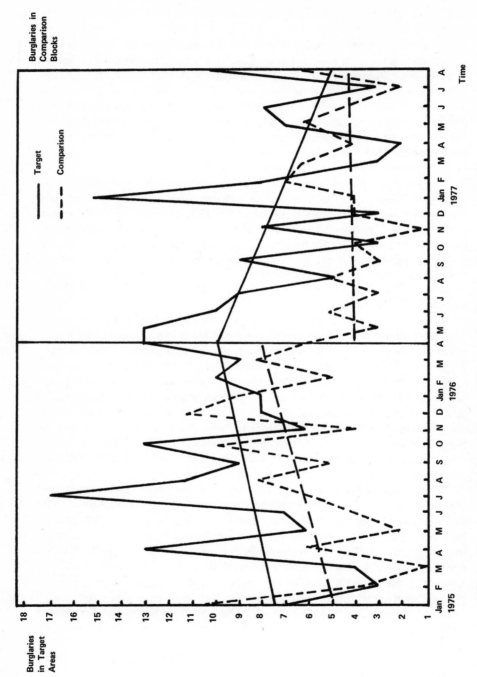

Figure 9-3. Burglaries in Target and Comparison Blocks (January 1975 to August 1977).

blocks. No *unique* decrease in burglary rates is observable among the blocks participating in the Neighborhood Watch component.

The trend lines drawn onto figure 9-3 deemphasize the instability present in both time series. As can be seen, there is considerably month-to-month variation in burglary levels. The general upward trend in both time series prior to April 1976 is marked by sharp differences in burglary levels on a month-to-month basis.

In the comparison time series, burglaries decrease during January and February 1976, increase in March, and then decline through May. Thereafter, they fluctuate around the trend line.

The target blocks experienced a general decline in reported burglaries from May 1976 through December 1976 (excepting reversals in September and November). In January 1977, however, burglaries jumped to preprogram levels, then declined through April 1977. Beyond that point, the burglary rates fluctuated around the trend line, reaching another high point during August 1977.

Program Impact in Selected Blocks. It is worthwhile focusing on the Neighborhood Watch blocks in more depth, to sort out any possible influencing variables that might have disguised or suppressed a measurable program impact. The analysis which is summarized here is presented primarily to examine in more detail rival hypotheses that could be offered as explanations for the lack of a measurable impact for burglary rates from the Neighborhood Watch blocks.

One variable which might have confounded the block-level comparison time series was whether a given comparison block was adjacent to a block organized into a Neighborhood Watch unit. It is possible that adjacent (nonprogram) blocks actually benefited from spillovers generated by organized blocks. A total of seventeen comparison blocks were within one block of a target block. These blocks were temporarily excluded from the analysis, and a line graph was prepared showing the burglary rates in the nonadjacent comparison blocks over time. The general trend in the preprogram series is very similar to that shown in figure 9-3. The peak in burglaries during the months prior to implementation of the program was very similar to that for all comparison blocks taken together. Burglaries drop from a preprogram high in December 1975 through the time the program was implemented and bottom out in May 1976. Beyond May, burglaries fluctuate around a trend line that is practically horizontal. In sum, exclusion of adjacent comparison blocks does not alter the general conclusion that the Neighborhood Watch component did not produce a unique decrease in reported burglaries at the block level.

Another rival hypothesis focuses on the point in the program at which the target blocks were organized. As was mentioned previously, the program coordinator who had taken the lead in implementing the Neighborhood Watch component and had been working with the block captains through the end of 1976 resigned his position. This event precipitated a lot of concern among block captains and suggests the hypothesis that those blocks organized early in the program would be better organized and more effective.

A total of thirty blocks (nearly half of all blocks organized) were organized during the first four months of the program. This effort was the most intensive one made. By taking these blocks and examining their reported burglaries over time, it is possible to see if there are any clear indications of program effectiveness.

Figure 9-4 displays the burglary rates in these thirty blocks before and after being organized as Neighborhood Watch units. Several features of the figure stand out. Prior to April 1976, the time series is very unstable. The predominant-trend line indicates an increase in burglaries through March 1976. Then a large increase occurs which coincides with the beginning of the program. From that point, burglaries decrease through August 1976, increase for September, and then decrease again. The large increase in reported burglaries in April 1976 and the subsequent decline might well be interpreted as the program having reduced burglaries. However, it is important to note that the jump in April is much like two other jumps that occurred *before* there was any program. Each of those peaks was followed by a sharp decrease in burglaries. The drop from April 1976 through August is likely to be another decrease of the same kind. It is worth noting, however, that the postimplementation time series for these thirty blocks suggests the possibility of a lasting impact more strongly than do the other target-block time series examined. With the exception of a one-month jump in September, burglary rates stay down until June 1977. This contrasts with the time series for all the target blocks, which jumps to preprogram burglary levels in January 1977.

Influence of Neighborhood Watch Units on Crime Reporting. Another issue illustrated by figure 9-4 has to do with predicted changes in reporting *rates* due to organization of city blocks. The systems diagram of the program (figure 8-1) hypothesizes that there will be a temporary increase in reports of burglaries as a result of more people reporting crimes they would not have reported before.

During each month between April and July, more blocks were organized: twelve by April 30, fifteen by May 31, twenty-six by June 30, and thirty by July 31. As these blocks were organized, it would be logical to expect a temporary *increase* in reported burglaries. But burglaries go *down* during that period. With the exception of a one-month increase in September, there

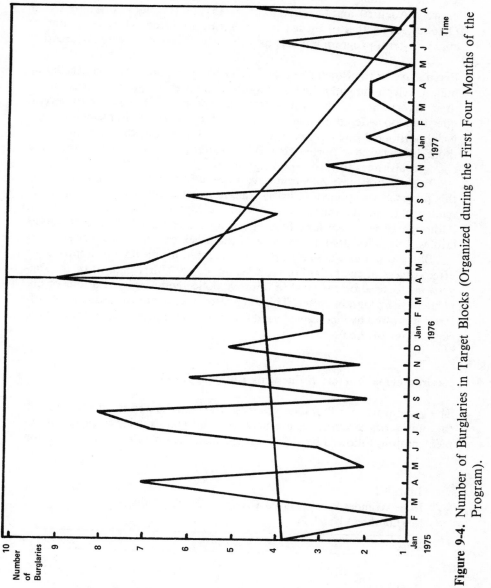

Figure 9-4. Number of Burglaries in Target Blocks (Organized during the First Four Months of the Program).

does not appear to be any discernible bulge in reported crimes *after* these blocks were organized either.

The remaining blocks were divided into two groups—those organized between August 1 and October 30 ($N = 15$) and the blocks organized after October 30. Neither of those two time series produced evidence of consistent short-term program impacts or a short-term reporting-rate differential.

Perspective of the Block Captains. Fifty block captains were contacted by mail or telephone and asked to respond to a series of questions focused on their perceptions of the crime-prevention program. Responses to several questions provide additional insight into the process of implementing the Neighborhood Watch component. Table 9-1 indicates that a majority of those interviewed reported that the Neighborhood Watch program had changed attitudes toward reporting crimes.

Table 9-2 displays *how* crime-reporting attitudes have been affected by this program component. Clearly, one noticeable change is the (reported) tendency to notify the police or a block captain of crimes committed. Although twenty mentions focused on an increased willingness to report crimes, this is less than a majority of the block captains interviewed.

Block captains were also asked for suggestions on how to improve the effectiveness of the Neighborhood Watch units. Thirty percent of the suggestions focused on the need to improve police-community relations or implement the program better. This suggestion was the most frequent one offered, followed by a perceived need for more police patrol (15 percent of the suggestions offered).

Environmental Factors Influencing Burglary Rates

The general pattern that emerges from the analysis and is replicated in all the time series examined is an increase in burglaries prior to program implementation followed by a decrease through the time the crime-prevention

Table 9-1
Have Attitudes Been Changed Toward Crime Reporting by the Neighborhood Watch Program?

Response	Number	Percent
Yes	33	66.0%
No	12	24.0
Don't know	1	2.0
No response	4	8.0
Total	50	100.0%

Table 9-2

Changes in Attitudes as a Result of the Neighborhood Watch Component

Response	Number	Percent of Responses
More willing to report crimes to police/block captain	20	60.6%
More willing to get involved	7	21.2
Have had no crimes	2	6.0
More confident will get action from police	1	3.0
Attitudes were different but police failed to respond	2	6.0
Only block captain's attitude has changed	1	3.0
Total	33	99.8%

program operated. On the face of it, this pattern would argue for the program's effectiveness. But examination of program components suggests a different conclusion. In fact, the Neighborhood Watch units, representing the bulk of first-year program outputs, did not distinguish themselves in terms of burglary rates from a random sample of nonorganized city blocks. The newspaper publicity given to the program was probably not sufficient to modify burglary rates for the entire city. Few burglary-security surveys were done and only a small number of citizen-band reports were recorded. In sum, the crime-prevention program probably did not affect burglary rates in a major way.

The question, then, is what factors other than program components did affect burglary trends. Answering this question is difficult because environmental factors operate on burglary rates simultaneously. It is likely that several variables influenced burglary rates, and the task of sorting out which ones and in what magnitude can become a complex statistical exercise that goes well beyond the level of this discussion.

It is useful to consider several environmental variables that the program planner in York and the evaluation staff hypothesized would influence citywide burglary rates. Associations between such factors and burglary trends cannot be interpreted as direct causal linkages, but nevertheless they offer partial explanations for observed trends in reported burglaries.

Unemployment Levels

Figure 9-5 displays the association between citywide burglary rates and the percent unemployed. The expected direction of the association would be

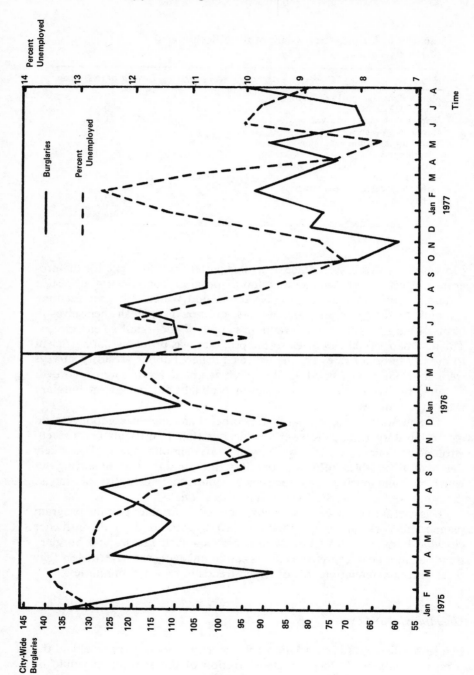

Figure 9-5. Citywide Burglary Rates and Percent Unemployed.

positive—as unemployment increases, so do burglaries. The correlation coefficient (explained in appendix A) is in fact positive ($r = .49$) for the entire time series. It is important to mention that prior to January 1976, unemployment rates were not calculated separately for the city of York, meaning that the data for the first twelve months in the time series are *estimates* supplied by the Bureau of Employment Security in York. The association from January 1976 through August 1977 appears to be stronger than that prior to January 1976, indicating a stronger influence on city burglary rates once unemployment is measured for York itself.

Other Environmental Variables

At least two other environmental variables could have substantially influenced burglary rates. The first was the unusually severe winter in the Northeast United States during 1976-77. Record low temperatures and snow falls in York could have reduced burglaries below the previous years' levels. The record high number of burglaries reported in December 1975 (figure 9-5) contrasts dramatically with the total reported in December 1976. The second factor could have operated to keep burglaries lower, once the winter had passed. In September 1976, a decision was made by the director of public safety to reorganize the Bureau of Police. The new organizational format emphasized the division of York into three geographic zones to be policed by teams of law enforcement officers who would be permanently assigned to one zone. Discussions with the Bureau of Police planner (also the crime-prevention planner) indicate that it took until March to iron out difficulties in the team-policing approach. From that point, team policing could have provided officers with increased familiarity with city neighborhoods, including the likely targets for burglaries. It is reasonable to hypothesize that burglaries could have been kept down by this higher deterrence level.

Neither of these variables is represented quantitatively in the data that comprise the basis for this evaluation. Measuring the effects of team policing per se would require an extension of the time series and would be facilitated by a change *back* to the traditional command structure. In fact, very recently, the chief administrative officer in the Bureau of Police has changed, and the new commissioner of police has decided to abolish team policing. An opportunity now exists to evaluate *that* organizational change and its influence on citywide burglary rates.

The severity of the winter could have been approximated by average monthly temperatures. This variable, graphed for the two winters represented in figure 9-5, might have been strongly associated with burglary rates.

The environmental variables examined in this evaluation do not exhaust the list of possible influences on burglary rates. It is likely that unemployment, together with other factors, did influence reported burglaries to produce the decline observed in the time series.

Regardless of how many environmental variables are considered, the main finding of this evaluation still stands. Since it was implemented, the crime-prevention program has not produced any measurable reduction in reported burglaries.

Conclusions and Recommendations

Conclusions

Analysis of linkages among program outputs, impacts, and environmental variables has pointed consistently to the conclusion that the crime-prevention program itself did not lead to reductions in burglary rates. Unemployment, as well as other (unmeasured) environmental variables, appeared to be more strongly associated with citywide crime trends than were program outputs. Crime trends in the blocks organized as Neighborhood Watch units did not behave much differently than those in nonorganized comparison blocks. Environmental factors are much less strongly associated with block-level trends, in part because of the month-to-month instability in these time series.

Burglary rates have been the focus of this evaluation. However, it is worth reporting that time series for property crimes do not suggest any findings that diverge from those reported in this book.

Examining levels of outputs from the program components suggests that an important problem was the low-level effort with respect to some components. The volunteer citizen-band emergency reporting network was responsible for some program outputs, but the small quantity of activities as well as the question of their crime-relatedness suggests that little impact could be expected from that component.

In terms of program effort, the security-surveys component was clearly deficient. The implementation objective of conducting such surveys in businesses and residences was not attained. The reasons for this failure in implementation are important. A lack of manpower presented an initial obstacle to the program planners, but resistance or a lack of interest on the part of residential dwellers constitutes an environmental constraint. Evidence suggests that that program component may not be implementable as it is formulated.

Environmental constraints as well as equity considerations resulted in substantial modifications to the original research design. Because the Neighborhood Watch component was targeted geographically, it was possible to utilize a multiple time-series design to evaluate the effectiveness of the Neighborhood Watch organizations.

The crime-prevention program, like most others implemented in a dynamic environment, influenced and was influenced by the systems of which it is a part. Because the program is an ongoing effort, it is important to offer recommendations that will improve the effective utilization of program resources.

Recommendations

1. More Neighborhood Watch units need to be created to encompass a greater proportion of the city's geographic areas. Organizing sixty-two blocks citywide represents only a very small proportion of the potential for Neighborhood Watch organizations. It is difficult to hypothesize a system-wide impact on crime trends until enough blocks are organized to significantly affect the perceived opportunities to commit property crimes in York. Equally important is the need to *sustain* contact with organized blocks. Effective crime prevention is a voluntary effort for block captains and city residents. Block captains who were interviewed tended to express dissatisfaction with the level of contact they had with the Bureau of Police beyond the initial organization phase on the blocks.

2. The home-security surveys component does not seem worth much additional effort. Interest appears to be small, and the likelihood of that kind of activity becoming widespread seems small. Security surveys of businesses could be emphasized, but for either type of survey it is important to distinguish between burglary-security surveys and codes-inspection surveys. Businessmen and residents are less likely to permit a security survey that is linked in their minds to citations for codes violations.

3. The entire program has to be more visible in the community. Although newspaper publicity was relatively extensive, it seems important to mount an effort to reach civic groups, business groups, schools, church organizations, and other institutions that would serve as a means to disseminate information. This would involve additional man-hours of public speaking time.

4. It is important to keep records that assist in evaluating the program's effectiveness. Existing measures of reported crimes kept by the Bureau of Police facilitated the evaluation a great deal. It was necessary, however, to gather the crime data for the comparison blocks by hand, utilizing incident reports filed during the 1975-1977 period. Data kept for the citizen-band reporting network did not facilitate evaluation of that component's effectiveness. In effect, the cause-effect assumptions that underlie the implementa-

tion of that component continue to go untested. It is worth noting that the grant-related requirements for effectiveness evaluations of crime-prevention programs such as the one in York are generally much less stringent than those incorporated in this particular evaluation. Indeed, the program implementation coincided with a reduction in burglaries, suggesting the program worked. More detailed data collection and analysis put together a different conclusion. That conclusion may engender some disappointment, but it is based on analysis that affords opportunities for program improvement.

5. Officers of the Bureau of Police are an important resource in an effective crime-prevention effort. To the extent that they can be enlisted to promote the components of the program as they do their jobs, the public will develop an image of a *police department* (and not just a crime-prevention officer) that is committed to the overall goal of preventing crimes. The core of crime prevention, motivating a community to participate in its own protection, is strengthened if its police officers behave in ways that convince residents that they are motivated to protect people and property.

10 Summary: Methodological Considerations

The preceding chapters have discussed the methods and results of three particular program evaluations as examples of the kind of program analytic efforts that might be most appropriately suited for small and medium-size cities. The purpose has been to point out methodological issues and approaches and in general to encourage greater interest in this kind of work in cities like Harrisburg, Williamsport, and York.

The three studies presented in this book provide a useful set of cases in terms of their similarities as well as their differences. While every program evaluation is unique to some extent, given the specifics of the program and its environment, these cases illustrate several types of problems and research-design considerations which are common to many evaluation efforts. This chapter begins by discussing some factors which may constrain the kind of research approach taken in these studies and then summarizes some of the main features of this type of evaluation as they relate to the valid and useful interpretation of results. Modifications of the research designs are suggested where appropriate to show how the validity of the findings could be improved.

Constraints on Evaluation

The low-effort, low-level research-design approach to program-effectiveness evaluation advocated in this book depends on making the greatest possible use of existing data and in general developing an evaluation strategy around a program in its "natural" setting rather than interfering with program implementation for primarily evaluation purposes. While some programs, particularly demonstration projects, lend themselves to some degree of experimental control, in these lower-level designs the design of the evaluation must be structured for the most part to accommodate features of program design and implementation rather than the other way around. In general, service delivery and managerial and political considerations take precedence over concerns for valid program evaluations. Studies designed and conducted in these circumstances, therefore, are likely to be more vulnerable to weaknesses and builtin biases in available sources of data and problems stemming from the way in which the program is implemented.

153

Adequacy of Existing Data Bases

While all types of evaluation designs must contend with problems of the quality of the data being analyzed, lower-level evaluations that rely more heavily on existing data bases may face data problems which by definition are beyond the evaluator's control. To the extent possible the evaluator should acquaint himself with the procedures used to collect the data he is considering using and the ways in which records are maintained and updated.

The quality of existing data bases which might be used in effectiveness evaluations—such as program-management data, records maintained in city hall, and various other secondary data sources—varies widely. In the Harrisburg housing-rehabilitation evaluation, for example, the routine program data maintained at the site offices were found to be incomplete and sometimes inconsistent. These data lacked a high degree of reliability and resulted in many missing values in the analysis. Whether the gaps and inconsistencies reflect systematic biases, a tendency to undercount renter-occupied dwelling units, for instance, is difficult to discern. Similar problems plagued other data sources considered for but not used in the housing evaluation, such as the Polk *City Directory* or *Profile of Change* data.

The evaluation of the York Crime-Prevention Program hinged on the use of Bureau of Police crime statistics as an indicator of crime trends over time. In general, these data appeared to be highly reliable as far as the accuracy of record-keeping procedures is concerned. On the other hand, their validity is questionable inasmuch as the number of crimes reported to the police in general is known to undercount all crimes committed. Yet these data were selected for use as the key dependent variables in this evaluation, in part because the gap between crimes reported and crimes committed was thought to be fairly uniform in different areas of York, but also in large part because first-hand victimization-survey data would have been much more costly and difficult to obtain. A further validity concern with these data is that the reporting rate itself was expected to increase as blocks became organized. This effect may have occurred, but existing evidence indicates that it was not a serious problem.

The Williamsport case differs from the other two inasmuch as the initial evaluation of the transit system and the development of the new service plan depended for the most part on primary data. Existing data were helpful in some respects—such as examining the financial picture and the maintenance program—but the most important sources of information were the boarding and alighting survey, the rider-interview survey, and the community telephone survey.

The evaluation of the effectiveness of the new system was, however, based on routinely collected data which were readily accessible. This time-series analysis examined trends on a monthly basis in a number of key indicators, all of which are tabulated by the Williamsport Bureau of Transportation on a regular basis for managerial and control purposes. While there were some reliability problems with the way certain variables, such as number of senior citizens, were tabulated, for the most part appropriate indicators for an extended time-series analysis were readily available from the bureau's records. These data were complemented to some extent by comparative-survey data concerning distances walked to and from bus stops and passengers' ratings of the service. The evaluation would have benefited further if data on waiting times had been available for the old and new service plans. In addition, it would have been helpful to have had data on transfers for a substantially longer preprogram period than was actually the case.

Importance of the Implementation Plan

Although the crime-prevention program was originally conceived of as a quasi-experiment and the housing program was not, as it turned out, both these evaluations were limited by the ways in which the programs were implemented. A major concern here, of course, is that if there is a general *lack* of implementation, it will be impossible to test the underlying logic of the program, a problem discussed later in this chapter. A lesser, but still significant, problem is that when, where, and how a program is implemented also can limit the scope of the evaluation.

Specifically, with respect to the Harrisburg Housing-Rehabilitation Program, although actual service delivery appears to differ somewhat between the two site offices, in general the same basic program was implemented in the two target areas. Furthermore, the same basic program was extended to the second-year areas. Thus there is very little variation in program operation which can be used as the basis for examining differential effects of varying program strategy. This is also true of the crime-prevention program, although in that evaluation it is probably less problematic.

When the Harrisburg Housing-Rehabilitation Program evaluation approach was being developed, the idea of building alternative treatments into the program was promoted. The idea was that if alternative loan and grant arrangements could be tried out, or if for example, a strict codes-enforcement effort could be mounted in one area without a rehabilitation program or with a reduced rehabilitation effort, such comparisons could be evaluated to gain further insight as to what strategies or combinations of strategies are most effective. This kind of comparison is not possible as the program has been implemented to date. However, changes in strategy may still be possible as the program moves to new areas in subsequent years.

A different type of problem was encountered in the crime-prevention evaluation. Originally, two components of the program (security surveys and Neighborhood Watch) were intended to be operationalized in selected census tracts and not offered to other counterpart tracts that were to serve as the comparison-group observations in the evaluation. Because residents in certain blocks within the comparison tracts demanded the program, this arrangement became politically infeasible as can well be understood. Therefore, the program was made available to blocks expressing an interest, violating the original evaluation approach. The evaluation strategy had to be tempered according to the realities of program implementation.

In Williamsport, the nature of the transit-improvement program—its being implemented on an areawide basis—also set constraints on the evaluation approach. The lack of legitimate comparison areas—sectors not targeted for improved services—virtually dictated a simple before-and-after or time-series design. In addition, the fact that the implementation of the new plan was a one-shot pervasive change rather than one that was phased in gradually over a longer time period served to facilitate either of these longitudinal approaches.

The Search for Comparison Areas

Stemming in large part from the ways in which programs are implemented is the difficulty of finding adequate comparison groups for quasi-experimental evaluations. Since certain cases usually become part of the program selectively—on the basis of need, interest, professional judgment, or whatever—other cases which might be available for comparison may well not be comparable. This problem may be especially pertinent when the "cases" participating in a city program are large areal units.

In the evaluation of the Harrisburg Housing-Rehabilitation Program, for example, there clearly were problems in finding a good comparison neighborhood or neighborhoods. In part, it may be that insufficient thought was given to the criteria for selecting a comparison area, but beyond this, there did appear to be a lack of candidate neighborhoods, areas with similar housing characteristics and demographic and socioeconomic trends, where redevelopment or related kinds of programs had not been in effect.

In the York Crime-Prevention Program evaluation, the intended comparisons between groups of census tracts were "contaminated" by some blocks being organized in the nonprogram areas, as mentioned earlier. In other respects, the tracts differed somewhat in the demographic characteristics of their populations. In any case, as the analysis shifted to the block as the unit of analysis rather than the census tract, the selection of comparison groups—now comparison blocks—was facilitated because there were many more blocks to choose from. Even though some comparison blocks that are contiguous with organized blocks might have been contaminated by the Neighborhood Watch component, this was adjusted for by examining the noncontiguous comparison blocks separately.

Interpreting Results

The problems just discussed notwithstanding, two of the studies presented in this book reflect some general issues surrounding the interpretation of results, which is really at the heart of the valid assessment of program effectiveness. Both the housing-rehabilitation and crime-prevention evaluations incorporate research strategies which strengthen the ability to interpret findings, but in both cases some questions are not fully answered. Furthermore, all three cases illustrate the need for a close familiarity with the substance of program and environment and the importance of judgment in evaluating a program's results.

The Issue of External Comparisons

The greatest issue in the interpretation of observed results is whether or not apparent effects can fairly be attributed to the program as opposed to some outside influence. One way to examine this issue is to base the evaluation on comparisons between program and no-program observations, which can lead to very different conclusions from those which might result from looking only at cases involved in the program. This approach is particularly useful where environmental factors may have influenced impact variables, confusing the issue of program effectiveness. In the housing and crime-prevention evaluations reported here, the comparison groups were comparison areas, and while there are problems in finding adequate comparison areas, as mentioned earlier, in both cases the evaluations are strengthened by the ability to gauge what might have happened if the program had *not* been put into effect.

The external comparison was particularly important in the crime-prevention evaluation, since an examination of the organized blocks' time series alone clearly would have corroborated the underlying program logic and probably would have led to misleading conclusions. The trend of increasing burglaries in the preprogram series and decreasing numbers of burglaries in the postprogram series would make it appear that the program had the anticipated impact on crime rates. Yet the fact that the overall decrease in burglaries over the same time period was even greater in the comparison blocks not receiving the program made it clear that some other influence easily could be responsible for the observed results.

External comparisons with nonprogram areas also strengthened interpretations in the housing-rehabilitation program evaluation. With respect to direct effects, the finding that the number of building permits rose substantially during the program year in the two target areas while remaining at their normal level in the comparison area provided a clearer indication that the program was actually responsible for some degree of change in the target areas. In terms of subsequent impacts, the comparison data on tax delinquencies and property transaction prices seem to indicate that the program had some positive value along these lines, but the data are preliminary and such conclusions are tentative at best.

In Williamsport, the sole reliance on the single-time-series approach precludes the use of external comparisons. This is not a serious problem in this case because no other rival explanations for the observed effects have suggested themselves. However, one way of corroborating the conclusion that the new system was effective would be to compare the trends in Williamsport with those in similar cities elsewhere in Pennsylvania. If similar trends did appear in cities without recent transit-improvement programs, then the ridership growth in Williamsport could not be attributed to the program. While these data were not available for other cities at the time this evaluation was conducted, they should be available shortly from PennDOT and can be used in the continuing monitoring of the Williamsport Bureau of Transportation's operation.

Process Linkages

The systems approach of linking effects to program process proved useful in all three evaluations as a way of understanding findings about the degree to which the anticipated results did or did not materialize. As it happened, in both the housing and crime-prevention cases, the process monitoring showed that a specific part of the program design was not really working. In both cases there evidently was a poor fit of program design to environment. In Williamsport, on the other hand, implementation was complete, and therefore the process linkages did materialize in the data analysis.

In the crime-prevention program, very few home security inspections were actually carried out, apparently because homeowners were not receptive to the idea. In the housing-rehabilitation program, the loan features have been utilized infrequently, although they had been expected to provide a strong incentive to property owners to make needed repairs. The finding that they evidently were not very attractive to many property owners whose properties were out of codes compliance is one explanation why participation in the rehabilitation program was less than anticipated.

Furthermore, the tracking of program outputs may provide comparisons which can help explain intermediate results and program effectiveness. For example, the results of initial housing inspections reveal a pattern of estimated costs of repairs which appears to influence whether property owners participated in the program.

Impacts of Environmental Factors

In addition to the linking of observed effects to program-operation variables and outputs, the importance of incorporating environmental factors into the evaluation cannot be overlooked. Environmental variables sometimes can result in changes which might be mistaken for program effects, and they can also serve to counteract real program effects. If the relevant environmental factors can be anticipated in a systems analysis, it may be possible to include them in data collection and make adjustments for their possible effects to aid in interpreting the real effects of the program. Failure to take them into account can produce very misleading results.

In the analysis of the survey data in the housing-rehabilitation evaluation, for example, the race variable was taken into account in comparing attitudes between respondents from program and nonprogram areas. In some instances these interpretations were quite different from what they would have been if race had been ignored. Other portions of the analysis could have benefited from similar use of other environmental variables. For example, in the analyses of participation in the rehabilitation program and of property transaction prices, it would have been helpful to take such factors as size of structure or number of rooms into consideration. However, this information was missing for many of the properties in the site-office files and thus could not be included in the analysis. Without this information, the findings are open to rival interpretations.

In the crime-prevention evaluation, the finding that there was a greater decrease in burglaries in the comparison blocks indicated that some environmental factor or factors must have exerted influence on crime rates. Without being able to identify the most likely of these factors and take them into account, the interpretations are less than satisfactory because the question of what caused the decreases is unanswered. Incorporating variables such as season and unemployment rate into the analysis provided greater insight as to what the effects of the program really were, but they still could not account for the overall citywide decrease in crime rate.

In the case of Williamsport, no environmental variables were dealt with explicitly. This was not felt to be necessary because those individuals who were familiar with the transit system and the community in general were not aware of anything besides the improvement program which conceivably could have produced the observed effects. If there had been any such environmental shifts, they would have to be taken into account to determine whether the apparent effectiveness of the program holds up.

Assessing Program Failure

A central theme in this book is the need to explain why programs fail to produce their intended effects. Frequently, evaluations produce mixed results, and the problem is to determine why the program is not more effective. As discussed earlier, tracking back to the examination of outputs is a way to determine whether the reason is basically a failure in theory or failure in program. While this is often a relatively straightforward issue, it can become highly judgmental—the question is how much program effort is enough to provide a fair test of the underlying program logic.

In the crime-prevention program, far fewer blocks were organized than might have been anticipated; only scattered blocks in the target census tracts became part of the program. Thus, when an analysis of crime statistics on a tract basis did not indicate that the program had produced any unique impact, the natural inclination was to conclude that the lack of effectiveness was due to a failure in program implementation. A reasonable rejoinder to such a conclusion is that if those blocks which were organized were those with the greatest need (high crime rates), then the program was implemented on a broad enough basis to test the program logic, and that the intended results would materialize in at least those blocks.

Such a rejoinder really throws open the issue of whether an apparent lack of effects is due to a failure in the underlying "theory" or whether the "theory" was really tested. In different words, two different theories could be involved in the block-organization component of the program. The first theory is that once a large enough proportion of blocks in a census tract has been organized, then an areawide deterrent effect emerges which results in a reduction in the areawide crime rate. The lack of any measurable program effect in the target tracts, given the small number of blocks organized, indicates that this theory may not have been fairly tested. The second theory, implicit in the rejoinder just mentioned, is that organizing blocks will result in a measurable drop in crime levels on those blocks. The block-level analysis included in the crime-prevention evaluation was a more valid test of this second theory.

If more blocks are organized as has been indicated in the second-year application for funding for the crime-prevention program, then a test of the first theory may well be feasible at the end of one more year of program operation.

The issue of failure in theory versus failure in program also surfaced in the housing-rehabilitation evaluation. The program was slow in gearing up, and implementation was uneven, which might lead one to conclude that a failure in program had occurred. On the other hand, the fact that virtually all houses had been inspected for codes violations in the initial target areas establishes that the program had been implemented. The survey (1977) confirmed that people in the initial area were aware of the existence of the program. Furthermore, those surveyed were generally aware that rehabilitation funds were available to bring their homes into compliance with city codes. Thus it seems fair to conclude that in this case, the theory was fairly tested.

Incentives offered by the program were not capable of inducing the majority of property owners to meet codes standards. The basic interpretation is that the environment was less receptive to the program than was expected, and that the strategy on which the program is based is only moderately effective.

The Williamsport case again stands in contrast to the other two studies in that there was a very clearcut and thorough implementation of the new routes and schedules along with the supporting recommendations. Thus the situation here did provide for a fair test of the logic stating that an improved service plan and auxiliary changes would produce a substantial increase in ridership. If the increase in ridership and the other anticipated impacts failed to materialize, it could not be attributed to a *failure of program*; rather, it would have to be a *failure of logic*, at least as it applies to the Williamsport context.

Summary

Program evaluations, even with much more sophisticated designs than those employed here, rarely provide complete explanations of their findings and total certainty in their conclusions. There are always problems in applying sound research methodology in an action setting, and some degree of selective judgment will usually be required in interpreting results. Problems were incurred in the three case studies included in this book in terms of collecting adequate and reliable data, using external no-program comparisons, and accounting fully for the influence of environmental variables. Unexpected deficiencies in the implementation of two of these programs further hindered the evaluators' ability to clearly assess the validity of the underlying program logic.

Nevertheless, with relatively low-effort approaches, these three evaluations did produce basically sound conclusions about the effectiveness of the particular programs. Furthermore, they were able to link observed strengths and weaknesses in outcomes with selected features of program design and implementation, thereby identifying reasons for underachievement and suggesting recommendations for improving performance. These cases, then, do illustrate the type of information about programs which can be developed by relatively low-effort formative evaluations. The extent to which undertaking such evaluations is worth the cost for local governments is considered in the final chapter.

11 Conclusions: Feasibility, Cost, and Utilization of Evaluations

This book has been concerned primarily with the application of legitimate research methods to formative evaluations of local governmental programs. It has pointed out methodological problems as well as advantages in the low-effort approaches employed here. The case studies illustrate that even with the inherent difficulties in low-level designs, they can be used to develop information which sheds light on program operations and suggests ways of improving performance. Given the potential of this kind of evaluation from a methodological perspective, then, concern centers around the issues of the feasibility and cost of conducting such studies and their general usefulness to local government.

Feasibility

The feasibility of low-effort program evaluations for smaller cities is clearly an important issue. Three specific concerns comprise the issue of feasibility: the extent to which cities maintain inhouse capabilities to conduct program analyses from start to finish, the issue of objectivity in analyses conducted by program managers, and the interest of managers/city officials in conducting the kinds of evaluations in this book. Each case study is useful in addressing these issues.

Inhouse Capabilities

Program evaluations of the kind discussed here require an effort that goes beyond routine program management and planning. An important question that needs to be raised is how much of the program-evaluation effort that is necessary can be made by planners, line managers, their staffs, and other city personnel.

None of the three program evaluations discussed in this book rely on advanced statistical techniques. The main technique used to present findings in the housing-rehabilitation evaluation is cross-tabulations of process and/or impact variables. Inspection of the marginal and cell percentages in these cross-tabulations yields information necessary to ascertain what effects, if any, the program has had. The transit-improvement evaluation and

163

the crime-prevention evaluation both rely on line graphs displaying output and impact measures over time. Visual inspection of these graphs, which is facilitated by the use of predominant-trend lines to characterize the trends before and after the programs were implemented, yields evidence of effectiveness.

Data Gathering. Much of the data for the crime-prevention evaluation were available from existing records of reported crimes. The Bureau of Police in York has recently converted to a computerized records system, which should enhance the data-collection capabilities of the police planner and his staff. Records maintained by the crime-prevention coordinator for program management and reporting purposes (the Governor's Justice Commission requires program-performance measures to support grant renewals) were useful in assessing levels of program outputs. The survey of block captains required a minimum of effort as measured in man-hours.

The transit-improvement evaluation in Williamsport relied on data collected as part of routine program operations as well as survey data collected especially for the evaluation. The one-day rider survey, the two-week operating-data survey, the geographically targeted surveys, and the postcard survey all required special efforts on the part of evaluation staff and city employees.

Data for the housing evaluation also required more effort to collect than for the crime-prevention evaluation. Although existing data sources were used to obtain measures of program outputs and some impacts, special efforts were made to collect these data in a form useful for the evaluators. In addition, survey data were collected before and after the program was implemented. Although neither set of survey data was very time-consuming to collect, additional personnel were used (city interns, research assistants).

In general, the data-collection phase of the evaluations (including coding and key punching) reported in this book are well within the capabilities (skills) of existing program personnel. The man-hours required to collect data that are not routinely collected by program personnel might be made available by using city interns.

Data Analysis. At issue, rather, is the capability of program personnel to analyze the data and interpret findings which bear upon program effectiveness. Although it is clear that many small and medium-size cities do not have the resources to employ people with the skills necessary to conduct the analyses presented here, it is likely that many other cities do in fact employ such people. The position taken here is that the methodologies used in the three case studies in this book could be adapted by program personnel in other cities. (It should be noted that the design for evaluating a housing-rehabilitation program in the city of York is similar to the one employed in

Harrisburg and discussed in this book. In York, the evaluation is being conducted by Department of Community Development staff.)

To the extent that this book serves as an exemplar to cities willing to undertake evaluations, it can suggest ways of analyzing data to measure program effectiveness. But particular cities, as they conduct program evaluations, will encounter data-analysis "puzzles" that were not anticipated in this discussion. Some cities will be able to resolve those puzzles by relying on the skills of inhouse personnel. Others will need outside technical assistance to guide efforts to analyze and interpret their program data. The methodology for calculating and interpreting predominant-trend lines, for example, may require the use of an outside consultant for a limited period of time.

Another issue that bears on the capability of cities to undertake evaluations is the time and commitment of resources necessary to complete such studies. Program managers in the case-study cities cited constant or decreasing operating budgets as an important constraint on manpower and other evaluation-related resources. The crime-prevention planner expressed a willingness to reevaluate the program, but mentioned decreases in Bureau of Police clerical personnel as well as his own increased workload as factors limiting his ability to undertake a reevaluation inhouse. Housing-rehabilitation planners did not have slack resources either, but expressed a willingness to conduct their own evaluation, *if* the results could be fed into an ongoing program. In other words, formative evaluations that could make a real contribution to future program management were viewed more favorably than summative evaluations. As a matter of course, the transit managers are engaged in further followup evaluations at this time.

Objectivity

Program managers as evaluators wear several hats. They are expected by their department heads and mayors to operate programs in a smooth fashion. Evidence of program success is usually beneficial for all concerned. Their own performance evaluations may be linked to how well programs for which they have responsibility are operating. As program evaluators, they are expected to exercise their judgment to develop balanced, objective assessments of program performance. This may be difficult, given expectations of their superiors and their own personal involvement in the program.

Program managers for the housing-rehabilitation program expressed a willingness to do an objective evaluation, but pointed out that the program was identified with the city administration and the mayor, and negative findings could generate adverse political consequences. In York the situation was different. The police planner did not think negative findings would be detrimental to his or the administration's well-being. But he cited his own closeness to the program as a reason for not doing the evaluation himself. In fact, he suggested that an inhouse evaluation after one year's operation would be easier from that standpoint than one after three years' operation.

Interest in Evaluations

A factor that is as important as inhouse capabilities or objectivity in determining the feasibility of evaluations is the *interest* in and commitment to doing program evaluations. Although increasing numbers of federal and state grants require evaluations, these are usually concerned with monitoring program implementation. Rates at which grant monies are expended and quantities of program outputs are generally required for such evaluations. Measures of program impacts, used in all three case studies, are seldom required. From program managers' perspectives, interest in doing effectiveness evaluations will be affected by two factors: the costs involved and the benefits (utility) derived from the analyses. Although it is clearly not possible to state ranges of costs for all types of program evaluations conducted in small or medium-size cities, costs for the three examples in this book can be estimated.

Costs

Tables 11-1 through 11-3 display estimated costs of conducting the three program evaluations in this book. All three tables estimate the cost of staff time required as well as the amount of computer time necessary to analyze the data. It is important to note that the staff-time component for other cities could vary from the estimates, depending on the amount of technical assistance involved.

The size of each program, measured in terms of dollars expended, is a point of contrast. The housing-rehabilitation program had expended approximately $128,000 to the time the evaluation was completed. It should be noted that this figure represents only a fraction of the total Community Development Grant funds Harrisburg has received to date.

In Williamsport, no new program was implemented. Instead, an existing transit system was modified and the modifications evaluated. The total budget for the Bureau of Transportation for 1977 was in the neighborhood of $682,200, which can be used in lieu of program funds expended.

Table 11-1
Estimated Costs for the Harrisburg Housing-Rehabilitation Evaluation

	Hours	Cost (Dollars)
1. 1975 Survey—Allison Hill		
Questionnaire design	(1 staff-day)	66[a]
Questionnaire preparation	6	18
Surveying	80	240
Coding	15	45
Key punching	5	20
Deck setup	(2 staff-days)	132
Subtotal		521
2. 1977 Survey		
Questionnaire design	(2 staff-days)	132
Questionnaire preparation	10	30
Surveying	188	564
Coding	40	120
Key punching	10	40
Deck setup	(2 staff-days)	132
Subtotal		1,018
3. Site-office program data		
Collection (includes coding)	81	243
Key punching	17	68
Deck setup	(2 staff-days)	132
Subtotal		443
4. Secondary data collection		
Building permits	4	12
Tax delinquencies	40	120
Transaction prices	40	120
Vacancy and migration	1	3
Preparing Polk data for use	8	24
Subtotal		279
5. Computer costs		
Data processing	1/2	288[b]
Printing output (20,000 lines)		64[b]
Subtotal		352
6. Data analysis and report writing		
Staff work	(10 staff-days)	660
Reproduction		200
Subtotal		860
Total		$3,473

[a]Estimated costs for staff time are based on an annual salary of $16,170. That annual salary amounts to an hourly rate of $8.25.

[b]These costs are based on The Pennsylvania State University's commercial rate.

Table 11-2
Estimated Costs for the Williamsport Transit-Improvement
Program Evaluation

	Hours	Cost (Dollars)
1. On-board surveys		
Questionnaire design	(3 staff-days)	198[a]
Questionnaire preparation	32	96
Surveying	320	960
Coding	100	300
Key punching	50	200
Deck setup	(1 staff-day)	66
Subtotal		1,820
2. Community survey		
Questionnaire design	(2 staff-days)	132
Questionnaire preparation	24	72
Surveying	100	300
Coding	20	60
Key punching	40	160
Deck setup	(1 staff-day)	66
Subtotal		790
3. Internal management study		
Review of management practices	(3 staff-days)	198
Tabulation of maintenance records	24	72
Subtotal		270
4. Financial analysis		
Data coding	16	48
Key punching	10	40
Deck setup	(½ staff-day)	33
Subtotal		121
5. Operations survey		
Check rides	60	180
Reliability checks	(2 staff-days)	132
Data tabulation	30	90
Subtotal		402
6. Computer costs		
Data processing	1	576[b]
Printing output (40,000 lines)		128[b]
Subtotal	704	704
7. Data analysis and report writing		
Staff work	(40 staff-days)	2,640
Reproduction		480
Subtotal		3,120
Total		$7,227

[a]Estimated costs for staff time are based on an annual salary of $16,170. That annual salary amounts to an hourly rate of $8.25.

[b]These costs are based on The Pennsylvania State University's commercial rate.

Table 11-3
Estimated Costs for the York Crime-Prevention Evaluation

	Hours	Cost (Dollars)
1. Survey of block captains		
Questionnaire design	(½ staff-day)	33a
Questionnaire preparation	3	9
Surveying	13	39
Coding	4	12
Subtotal		93
2. Collecting of block-level crime data		
Data collection	50	150
Coding	35	105
Key punching	4	16
Deck setup	(1 staff-day)	66
Subtotal		337
3. Computer costs		
Data processing	1/2	288b
Printing output (5,000 lines)		16b
Subtotal		304
4. Data analysis and report writing		
Staff work	(10 staff-days)	660
Reproduction		100
Subtotal		760
Total		$1,494

aEstimated costs for staff time are based on an annual salary of $16,170. That annual salary amounts to an hourly rate of $8.25.

bThese costs are based on The Pennsylvania State University's commercial rate.

The first-year cost of the crime-prevention program was $15,598. This is by far the smallest budget among the three programs evaluated. The relative costs of the three evaluations, $3,473 for the housing-rehabilitation evaluation, $7,227 for the transit-improvement evaluation, and $1,494 for the crime-prevention evaluation are somewhat closer in magnitude, indicating that regardless of program cost, it is necessary to expend sufficient funds to conduct an adequate evaluation. Although a minimum cost for the kind of program evaluation illustrated in this book is difficult to estimate, $1,000 is probably the minimum.

Expressed as a percentage of the funds expended, the cost of the housing-rehabilitation program evaluation was 2.7 percent. The comparable figure for the crime-prevention program evaluation was 9.6 percent, and for the transit-improvement program evaluation, 1.0 percent.

In general, then, the evaluations cost only a fraction of actual program costs and therefore can be considered a worthwhile investment, given useful results. In the case of Williamsport, moreover, the additional revenue earned by virtue of putting the new system into effect was much greater than the cost of the original study leading to the development of that new plan.

Utility

Each program evaluation in this book is set in a different context. The transit-improvement program was prompted by an obvious deterioration in the city-owned bus system. The need to do something was clear, but transit managers did not know how to pinpoint weaknesses or make changes to improve service and attract new ridership. The improvement program offered a set of recommendations for change which were implemented and proved to be effective in improving performance. Evaluating the improvement program (the case study in this book) affords an opportunity to fine tune the system.

The housing-rehabilitation program was intended to ameliorate an obvious problem of declining neighborhoods in Harrisburg. Reasons for deterioration were generally known, and the program logic was aimed at affecting some neighborhood trends that the city could reasonably expect to modify. The program evaluation produced findings concerning program deficiencies which planners and program managers had suspected were true, but the study sharpened their understanding of the problems and suggested strategies for improving performance.

In York, the crime-prevention program was prompted by a need to reduce burglary rates, and it implemented a program logic that was more experimental. Based in part on preprogram recommendations by the mayor's Council on Safe Streets, program components were implemented in an environment where their acceptability and effectiveness were open to question. The results of the evaluation pointed to the need to substantially modify the program logic.

Relevance of the Results

The overall utility of program-effectiveness evaluations to small and medium-size cities is difficult to determine. One criterion should be the results produced—did a given evaluation provide useful information? The type of analysis discussed in this book is aimed at determining whether or not programs are meeting their objectives. If the answers to such questions are not really known, then an evaluation which can arrive at definite conclusions with a strong degree of confidence should be worthwhile.

On the other hand, program evaluations are often criticized on the grounds that their results only serve to confirm the obvious, implying that managers already know a good deal about their programs' performance. To the extent that this is true, a formal evaluation may not have much to contribute and therefore would not be worth the effort. The problem with this point of view is that rather than confirming the obvious, many evaluations may be corroborating what has been suspected but not really tested. After the evaluation has been completed and the results turn out *not* to be full of surprises, the worth of the evaluation itself may seem pretty small, but if the results turn out to dispute the conventional wisdom or usual assumptions, the same evaluation effort may be seen as being fairly important. Frequently, conducting a program evaluation is not a matter of confirming program logic completely, but rather a refinement of the impressions which people close to the program have. Pinpointing more sharply the degree to which a program is proving effective and perhaps gaining additional insight as to the lack of success with certain cases is valuable information.

A major purpose of formative evaluations, especially those based on the linking of observed effects with an examination of program process, is to explain why programs are working or not working, or why they are working better in some circumstances than in others. This kind of finding can have considerable value if it suggests recommendations for improving the program's design or the way it is managed. Rather than a recommendation to continue or discontinue, adopt or discard the program, the real question which formative evaluations are concerned with is how can the program be improved. All three cases presented in this book do develop recommendations for improving program performance based on analysis of the way in which the respective programs have been implemented and their observed effectiveness up through the points in time when the evaluations were conducted. If these recommendations can be implemented and in fact do lead to improved performance, the evaluations would clearly be justified.

This raises the whole issue of utilization—are the recommendations that come out of evaluations given credence and put into practice? The track record on this issue has been generally poor to date for a variety of reasons. The first problem is that the quality of program evaluations has been uneven, with the result that recommendations have been developed which do not hold up under closer scrutiny, and this obviously has not helped the cause of evaluation. Second, there is often a lack of interest in evaluations, even when they are of high quality. They are looked upon as anything from outright interference with service delivery to pure academic exercises, but in any event are not given the opportunity to be utilized. In general, the utilization of results should also be a criterion for assessing the worth of program evaluation, but by this measure, many evaluations with inherent value probably have been underrated.

Utilization of Case-Study Recommendations

Recommendations from the three case studies were made with the intention of providing formative feedback to program managers. Follow-up discussions with housing-rehabilitation program personnel indicated that several evaluation recommendations have been implemented. The administration of the program has been modified so that one person is in charge of the entire program operation. This is consistent with the main thrust of Recommendation 5 in chapter 5. The Bureaus of Codes Administration and Planning share administrative responsibilities under the new program coordinator. Follow-up codes enforcement (suggested as part of Recommendation 1) is now being initiated in the initial target areas. The strategy is to notify all homeowners whose dwellings are out of compliance and are not being rehabilitated that they will be prosecuted. A grace period of two months is planned to allow owners to initiate repairs and take advantage of the rehabilitation program. When court proceedings begin, they will be targeted on blocks with dwellings obviously out of compliance. The demonstration effect of prosecution is intended to spur participation of people in the expanded areas in the program. Where codes inspections are continuing (in the newer areas of the program), inspectors have been instructed to emphasize repair of major structural and safety violations first. This too is consistent with another part of Recommendation 1 in chapter 5.

The crime-prevention program is now in its third year of operation. Since April 1978, the program, under the management of a new program coordinator, has devoted considerable effort to rebuilding. Prior to that point, there had been no coordinator for a six-month period, resulting in very little crime-prevention effort. Several changes in the direction of the program stem from evaluation recommendations.

Currently, many of the blocks that had been organized as part of the first-year Neighborhood Watch effort are being reorganized. Emphasis is being placed on developing stronger relationships between block captains and the Bureau of Police. Some new blocks are also being organized to broaden the impact of the Neighborhood Watch component. Recommendation in chapter 9 suggests these changes.

Little effort is being devoted to security surveys (Recommendation 2), and much more effort is being targeted on mass-media publicity and civic participation (Recommendation 3). In July 1978, a York City Crime Prevention Council was established. In addition to the crime-prevention coordinator, membership includes twenty-five representatives of civic and community-based organizations. Monthly meetings are held to explain crime prevention and encourage representatives to distribute literature to their own organizations.

The transit-improvement evaluation generated a number of specific recommendations aimed at fine tuning the transit system's operations. The recommendations were accepted by the system's management, and at the time of this writing plans are being made to introduce these further changes in the system's operation over the next few months.

Concluding Comments

The potential worth of a given program-effectiveness evaluation is a judgmental matter. This book is intended to stimulate increased interest in and usage of evaluations, but more specifically the *selective* use of effectiveness evaluations where they have some utility. In general, the level of effort should be tailored, as much as is possible before the fact, to the need for information and the probable difficulty in measuring effects and isolating the underlying cause-effect relationships. Where the nature of the findings is clearly in doubt and where the probability of environmental influences is high—where there are likely rival explanations—a more structured research design is appropriate. In other situations, where fewer plausible rival hypotheses exist, the research approach may be more simple and less costly, and more feasible for cities with minimal staff resources or limited analytical capabilities.

In summary, then, the utility of program evaluations for small and medium-size cities varies widely depending on the program, its environment, the state of existing knowledge about its effectiveness, the ability to design and conduct an inhouse evaluation, and the interest and commitment of the city in building evaluation into overall planning/programming processes. The three case studies presented in this book were relatively low-cost efforts which produced clearcut findings and conclusions that were useful to decision makers, as demonstrated by the extent to which their recommendations have been implemented. In some small and medium-size cities, where the analytical capability is available, such skills should be applied more frequently in effectiveness evaluations relative to other kinds of analytical efforts.

In cities without these capabilities, more thought should be given to developing them on an inhouse basis and to seeking outside technical assistance so as to utilize effectiveness evaluations in instances where there is clearly a potential for improving program performance. There clearly is a need for good information on program performance in varied service areas—this book illustrates the kind of low-effort evaluations which are most likely to be feasible in small and medium-size cities and yet capable of producing valid results. Their utility rests on the willingness of cities to undertake these efforts, the quality of the results generated, the utilization of the results, and ultimately, improved program performance.

Appendixes

Appendix A
Statistical Analysis of
Time-Series Data

Explanation of Predominant-Trend Lines

The predominant-trend lines used in both the transit-improvement and crime-prevention program evaluations are developed by fitting straight-line equations to the data in those time series. Such equations are called *linear-regression equations*.

Regression equations that summarize the linear association between two variables can be written as follows:

$$\hat{Y}_i = b_0 + b_1 X_i$$

In this book, the variable Y_i represents the output or impact variable that is being plotted over time. The variable X_i is time itself, expressed in regular intervals (usually months in the cases presented in this book). The notation b_0 represents a single number, called a *constant*. Its value, once the regression equation is calculated, is fixed. The notation b_1 is a *regression coefficient* which represents the extent to which the predominant-trend line (regression line) slopes upward or downward. If a regression line slopes upward (larger values of Y are associated with larger values of X), then b_1 has a positive value ($b_1 > 0$). Correspondingly, where the regression line slopes downward (larger values of Y are associated with decreases in X), b_1 is negative ($b_1 < 0$).

The special case where $b_1 = 0$ indicates that as X changes, there is *no change* in the output or impact variable being graphed. This indicates that there is *no association* between X_i and the Y_i variable. The graphs in figure A-1 illustrate regression lines. In both graphs the straight lines serve to "summarize" the data represented. Notice that the *actual* values of the Y_i variable are scattered around the regression lines. For each point in time, the difference between the *predicted value of Y* ($\hat{Y}_i$) and the *actual value of Y* (Y_i) is *error*. If the actual values of Y are clustered closely around the regression line (as illustrated in figure A-1), the straight-line equation does a good job of summarizing the actual association between the X_i variable and the Y_i variable. Such a situation is described as one where the two variables are *strongly associated*. On the other hand, if there is a lot of scatter around the line described by the regression equation, then the association between the two variables is *weak*. Although rare, there are instances where there is no scatter around the regression line; that is, all the data points fall right on the line. Such a situation would be described as a *perfect association* between

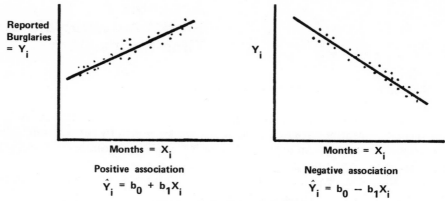

Figure A-1. Regression Lines.

X_i and Y_i. In different words, for each value of X_i, the straight-line equation predicts the exact value of Y_i.

An association can be positive (meaning the slope of the regression line is positive) or an association can be negative (negative slope). The strength of an association can be described with a statistic called the *correlation coefficient* (r). If the association is perfect, r will equal $+1$ (perfect positive association) or -1 (perfect negative association). Values for r can fall anywhere between $+1$ and -1. An $r = 0$ indicates no association between two variables.

The correlation coefficient also serves as the basis for another useful statistic. By squaring r, a statistic called the *coefficient of determination* (r^2) is created. This measure is useful to see how much of the variation in the values of Y_i can be explained from knowledge of corresponding values of X_i. Values of r^2 vary between 0 (knowledge of X_i does not explain any of the variation in Y_i) and 1 (knowledge of X_i perfectly explains the variation in Y_i).

There are three formulae which are useful in calculating the regression equation and the correlation coefficient. The formula for b_1 is

$$b_1 = \frac{\Sigma(X_i - \overline{X})(Y_i - \overline{Y})}{\Sigma(X_i - \overline{X})^2}$$

In words, this formula directs the researcher to subtract the arithmetic mean ($\overline{X}$) from each value of the variable X ($X_i - \overline{X}$) and multiply that difference by the corresponding difference between Y_i and $\overline{Y}$. The products of these differences are added together (Σ). In the denominator, each difference between X_i and $\bar{X}$ is squared, and then the squared differences are added together. Finally, the numerator is divided by the denominator to get the slope (b_1).

The value of b_0 (often called the *Y intercept*) is found by applying this formula:

$$b_0 = \bar{Y} - b_1\bar{X}$$

The value of the correlation coefficient (r) is determined by applying the following formula:

$$r = \frac{\Sigma(X_i - \bar{X})(Y_i - \bar{Y})}{\sqrt{\Sigma(X_i - \bar{X})^2\ \Sigma(Y_i - \bar{Y})^2}}$$

Note that the numerator of the formula for r is the same as for b_1. The denominator involves taking the difference of each X_i and Y_i from its mean, then squaring each difference. All the squared differences between X_i and $\bar{X}$ are summed, and all the squared differences between Y_i and $\bar{Y}$ are summed. Then the two sums are multiplied, and finally, the square root of the product is taken. The last step is to divide the numerator by the denominator.

Table A-1 illustrates the calculations that are necessary to compute a regression equation.

$Y = 5 + .19X_i$ was the regression equation used to create the predominant-trend line for the preprogram target block time series in figure 9-3. To draw in the straight line, two points on the line were calculated: $X_i = 13$ is the beginning point, and substitution of 13 for X_i in the regression equation yields a value $\hat{Y} = 7.47$; $X_i = 27$ is the end point of the preprogram series, and substitution of 27 for X_i yields a value $\hat{Y} = 10.13$.

In the crime-prevention evaluation presented in this book, regression techniques were also used to examine the association between program output variables (newspaper coverage) and impact variables (crime trends), as well as between environmental variables (unemployment) and impact variables. The analyses presented in this book were supplemented by regressions aimed at sorting out the relative influences of output and environmental variables on impact measures. Seasonal influences in crime trends were measured with a series of dichotomous variables sometimes referred to as *dummy variables*. The crime-prevention program itself was included as a dichotomous variable in selected analyses. In general, the results of these additional efforts corroborate the main conclusion that there was no unique impact attributable to the crime-prevention program components.

A more complete introduction to correlation and regression techniques

Table A-1
Computations to Calculate the Time-Series Regression Line

Burglaries in Target Blocks Y_i	Time[a] X_i	$(Y_i - \bar{Y})$	$(X_i - \bar{X})$	Covariation $(X_i - \bar{X})(Y_i - \bar{Y})$	Variation in X $(X_i - \bar{X})^2$	Variation in Y $(Y_i - \bar{Y})^2$
8	13	−0.8	−7	5.6	49	0.64
3	14	−5.8	−6	34.8	36	33.64
4	15	−4.8	−5	24.0	25	23.04
13	16	4.2	−4	−16.8	16	17.64
6	17	−2.8	−3	8.4	9	7.84
7	18	−1.8	−2	3.6	4	3.24
17	19	8.2	−1	−8.2	1	67.24
11	20	2.2	0	0.0	0	4.84
9	21	.2	1	0.2	1	0.04
13	22	4.2	2	8.4	4	17.64
6	23	−2.8	3	−8.4	9	7.84
8	24	−0.8	4	−3.2	16	0.64
8	25	−0.8	5	−4.0	25	0.64
10	26	1.2	6	7.2	36	1.44
9	27	0.2	7	1.4	49	0.04
$\Sigma Y_i = 132$	$\Sigma X_i = 300$	$\Sigma = 0$	$\Sigma = 0$	$\Sigma = 53$	$\Sigma = 280$	$\Sigma = 186.40$
$\bar{Y}_i = 8.8$	$\bar{X}_i = 20$					

$$b_1 = \frac{\Sigma(X_i - \bar{X})(Y_i - \bar{Y})}{\Sigma(X_i - \bar{X})^2} = \frac{53}{280} = .19$$

$$b_0 = \bar{Y}_i - b_1 \bar{X}_i = 8.8 - .19(20) = 5$$

$$\hat{Y} = 5 + .19X_i$$

$$r = \frac{\Sigma(X_i - \bar{X})(Y_i - \bar{Y})}{\sqrt{\Sigma(X_i - \bar{X})^2 \; \Sigma(Y_i - \bar{Y})^2}} = \frac{53}{\sqrt{(280)(186.4)}} = .24$$

$$r^2 = .06$$

[a]Values of X_i range from 13 upward because the entire time series begins in January 1974. Values for burglaries on the target blocks were available from January 1975, thirteen months from the point when the time series originated.

is presented in Theodore H. Poister, *Public Program Analysis: Applied Research Methods* (Baltimore: University Park Press, 1978), esp. chap. 14, pp. 509-534. Applications of these techniques to time series and consideration of special issues involved are discussed in the same text, pp. 572-580.

Deseasonalization of Time-Series Data

Since many of the variations associated with the operation of a transit system exhibit regular fluctuation on a seasonal basis, it is often helpful to adjust the data for the seasonal variation before computing predominant-trend lines and comparing pre-implementation and postimplementation series. The basic philosophy of this approach is to determine the extent to which the variables for a given month deviate from mean averages for the entire year and then adjust these variables accordingly.

The following example illustrates how the variable, passengers per day, was deseasonalized before it was graphed in figure 7-4. Table A-2 shows, for each of the four years in the transit-improvement program time-series analysis, the original (unadjusted) number of passengers per day on the system for each month. This includes all twelve months for 1975, 1976, and 1977, and January through September of 1978. For each year, the mean average computed across those months is also shown. The next column in each quadrant of the table shows *approximate index variables*, which are computed by dividing the value of the variable for each given month by the mean average for the year. For example, the approximate index value for January 1975 of 1.084 was computed by dividing the unadjusted variable 3,006 by the annual average of 2,774.

Once this has been done separately for each year, the approximate index variables for each month are averaged across the number of years in the complete time series. For example, the approximate index values for January—1.084, 1.025, .966, and .977—are summed and divided by four to yield the overall seasonal index of 1.013. In this example, the approximate index values are indexed across all four years for the months January through September and across only three years—1975, 1976, and 1977—for October, November, and December.

Finally, the original values of the variable, passengers per day, are deseasonalized by dividing each unadjusted value by the seasonal index value corresponding to that particular month. Following through in the example, this means that 3,006 would be divided by 1.013, yielding the deseasonalized value of 2,967. This process yields the set of deseasonalized values shown in the third column of the table. These deseasonalized values, then, are the data points which are shown in figure 7-4. For those months which consistently had more passengers per day than the annual mean average, this deseasonalization process has adjusted those values downward. Conversely, for those months which consistently had fewer passengers per day than the annual variation, deseasonalizing results in adjusting these values upward. Thus the deseasonalized values exhibit less

Table A-2
Computations for Deseasonalizing Passengers Per Day Variable

	Unadjusted Value	Approximate Index	Deseasonalized Value
1975			
January	3006	1.084	2967
February	2945	1.061	2921
March	2756	.994	2707
April	2629	.948	2605
May	2569	.926	2690
June	2675	.964	2721
July	2585	.932	2776
August	2561	.923	2632
September	2802	1.010	2847
October	2778	1.001	2814
November	2927	1.055	2779
December	3061	1.103	2808
Mean $(\bar{X})$ = 2774			
1976			
January	2868	1.025	2831
February	2868	1.025	2768
March	2859	1.022	2808
April	2991	1.069	2964
May	2764	.988	2894
June	2880	1.030	2929
July	2476	.885	2659
August	2673	.956	2747
September	2689	.961	2732
October	2642	.945	2676
November	2846	1.018	2702
December	3008	1.076	2759
Mean $(\bar{X})$ = 2797			
1977			
January	2698	.966	2663
February	2928	1.049	2826
March	2837	1.016	2786
April	2812	1.007	2786
May	2636	.944	2760
June	2567	.919	2611
July	2594	.929	2786
August	2854	1.022	2933
September	2664	.954	2707
October	2836	1.016	2873
November	3028	1.085	2875
December	3046	1.091	2794
Mean $(\bar{X})$ = 2792			
1978			
January	3067	.977	3027
February	3164	1.008	3054
March	3265	1.040	3207
April	3174	1.011	3145
May	3017	.961	3159
June	3203	1.020	3258
July	3070	.978	3297
August	3118	.993	3204
September	3171	1.010	3222
Mean $(\bar{X})$ = 3139			

Seasonal Index

January	1.013	May	.955	September	.984
February	1.036	June	.983	October	.987
March	1.018	July	.931	November	1.053
April	1.009	August	.973	December	1.090

variation than do the unadjusted values, as is seen by comparing the first and third columns in the table. This reduction in the amount of total variation represents the systematic month-to-month fluctuation which has been extracted from the data.

Follow-up Survey
Harrisburg Housing Rehabilitation Program

Case No. ____ ____Allison Hill ____Comparison Area   Case ____ ____ ____
                                                              C1   C2   C3

Address _____   Area
                                                              ____
        _____   C5

Number of Callbacks   1   2   3   4

Interviewer _____   Interviewer ____
                                                                  C6

Dwelling Type: Dwelling ____
                                                               C7
1 ____ Single-Family   2 ____ Duplex

3 ____ Row House   4 ____ Apartment

5 ____ Mixed-Occupancy

Sex: 1 ____ Male   2 ____ Female   Sex   ____
                                                               C8

Race: 1 ____ White   2 ____ Nonwhite   Race   ____
                                                               C9

Position in Household: 1 ____ Head   2 ____ Spouse   Position ____
                                                                 C10
                        3 ____ Other

   "I'd like to begin by asking you a few questions
about your neighborhood."

1. About how long have you been living in this
    neighborhood?

    _____Years   1.   ____ ____
                                                            C11 C12

2. If you had a choice, would you prefer to stay
    in this neighborhood or move?

    1 ____ Stay   2 ____ Move   3 ____ Don't Know/   2.   ____
                                        No Response   C14

185

3. Thinking of public services--such as fire and police protection, parks, transportation, trash collection, and street maintenance, do you think the services here in your neighborhood are generally better than in other parts of the City, about the same, or not as good as in other parts of the City?

   1 ___ Better   2 ___ Same   3 ___ Not as Good   3.   ____

                                                            C15

   4 ___ Uncertain   0 ___ Don't Know/No Response

4. What public services, if any, do you think should be improved in this neighborhood?

   a. _____ a.   ____   ____
                                                       C16   C17

   b. _____ b.   ____   ____
                                                       C18   C19

   c. _____ c.   ____   ____
                                                       C20   C21

   d. _____ d.   ____   ____
                                                       C22   C23

5. "Now I'm going to read you a list of statements, each of which refers to some aspect of the neighborhood where you live at this time. Indicate whether you agree or disagree with the following statements regarding your neighborhood. You can strongly agree, agree, feel neutral about the statement, disagree, or strongly disagree with it."

   | HAND INTERVIEWEE RESPONSE CARD. |

	Strongly Agree	Agree	Neutral	Disagree	Strongly Disagree	Don't Know/ No Response		
a. Properties in this neighborhood are well maintained.	5 ___	4 ___	3 ___	2 ___	1 ___	0 ___	a.	____ C24
b. This neighborhood is served with good recreational facilities.	5 ___	4 ___	3 ___	2 ___	1 ___	0 ___	b.	____ C25
c. A person is safe from crime in this neighborhood.	5 ___	4 ___	3 ___	2 ___	1 ___	0 ___	c.	____ C26

	Strongly Agree	Agree	Neutral	Disagree	Strongly Disagree	Don't Know/ No Response	

d. The streets and sidewalks in this neighborhood are in good condition.   5___ 4___ 3___ 2___ 1___ 0___   d. ___
C27

e. The housing in this neighborhood is in good condition.   5___ 4___ 3___ 2___ 1___ 0___   e. ___
C28

f. This neighborhood is becoming a less desirable place in which to live.   1___ 2___ 3___ 4___ 5___ 0___   f. ___
C29

g. Over the past 2 or 3 years, crime in this neighborhood has increased.   1___ 2___ 3___ 4___ 5___ 0___   g. ___
C30

h. The police provide good service to this neighborhood.   5___ 4___ 3___ 2___ 1___ 0___   h. ___
C31

i. This neighborhood is a good place in which to bring up children.   5___ 4___ 3___ 2___ 1___ 0___   i. ___
C32

j. This neighborhood is deteriorating fast.   1___ 2___ 3___ 4___ 5___ 0___   j. ___
C33

k. Over the past 2 or 3 years, housing conditions in this neighborhood have improved significantly.   5___ 4___ 3___ 2___ 1___ 0___   k. ___
C34

l. The City government is committed to improving

		Strongly Agree	Agree	Neutral	Disagree	Strongly Disagree	Don't Know/ No Response	
	the quality of this neighbor- hood.	5___	4___	3___	2___	1___	0___	l. ____ C35
m.	People in this neighborhood are taking better care of their homes than they were 2 or 3 years ago.	5___	4___	3___	2___	1___	0___	m. ____ C36
n.	The streets in this neighbor- hood are not well lighted at night.	1___	2___	3___	4___	5___	0___	n. ____ C37
o.	Abandoned houses and other empty buildings are a big problem in this neighbor- hood.	1___	2___	3___	4___	5___	0___	o. ____ C38
p.	The trash collec- tion in this neighborhood is poor.	1___	2___	3___	4___	5___	0___	p. ____ C39
q.	In general, this neighborhood is a better place in which to live than it was 2 or 3 years ago.	5___	4___	3___	2___	1___	0___	q. ____ C40
r.	Over the past 2 or 3 years, the number of abandoned build- ings in this neighborhood has increased.	1___	2___	3___	4___	5___	0___	r. ____ C41
s.	This neighborhood is visually attrac- tive, as compared with other neigh- borhoods in the City.	5___	4___	3___	2___	1___	0___	s. ____ C42

"The next set of questions pertains more directly to your home."

6. About how long have you been living in this
   house (or apartment)?   6. ____ ____
                                                           C43 C44

7. Do you own or rent this home (or apartment)?

   1 ___ Own Outright   2 ___ Buying

   3 ___ Renting   8 ___ Other   7.   ____
                                                               C46

   | IF RENTING, SKIP TO QUESTION 10. |

8. | IF OWN OR BUYING: | How satisfied are you
   with this home in meeting the needs of you and
   you family?

   1 ___ Very Satisfied   2 ___ Satisfied

   3 ___ Dissatisfied   4 ___ Uncertain

   0 ___ Don't Know/No Response   8.   ____
                                                               C47

9. What do you think has happened to the market
   value of this property over the past 3 years?

   1 ___ Increased   2 ___ Decreased

   3 ___ Stayed the Same   4 ___ Uncertain

   0 ___ Don't Know/No Response   9.   ____
                                                               C48

10. | IF RENTING: | How would you rate the condition
    of these premises?

    1 ___ Outstanding   2 ___ Good   3 ___ Fair

    4 ___ Poor   0 ___ Don't Know/No Response 10.   ____
                                                               C49

11. How would you rate your dealings with your landlord?

    1 ___ Very Good   2 ___ Good   3 ___ Fair

    4 ___ Poor   0 ___ Don't Know/No Response 11.   ____
                                                               C50

    | IF NOT EMPHASIS AREA, SKIP TO QUESTION 19. |

12. Are you aware of the housing rehabilitation
    program that the City has been conducting in
    this area?

    1 ___ Yes   2 ___ No   0 ___ No Response   12.   ____
                                                               C51

    | IF NO, SKIP TO QUESTION 19. |

13. | IF FIRST YEAR: | If yes: As you may know, this
program is almost completed in this area. How
satisfied are you with the way this program has
been carried out?

  1 ___ Very Satisfied   2 ___ Satisfied

  3 ___ Neutral   4 ___ Dissatisfied

  5 ___ Very Dissatisfied 0 ___ Don't Know/
                          No Response   13. ___
                                            C52

| IF SECOND YEAR: | If yes: As you may know, this
program has been going on for about 1½ years. How
satisfied are you with the way this program is
being carried out?

  1 ___ Very Satisfied   2 ___ Satisfied

  3 ___ Neutral   4 ___ Dissatisfied

  5 ___ Very Dissatisfied 0 ___ Don't Know/
                          No Response   13. ___
                                            C53

14. | IF NOT SATISFIED: | Why not? _____

_____

_____   14. ___ ___
                                            C54 C55

15. What do you think might have been done differently
to improve the program? _____

_____

_____   15. ___ ___
                                            C56 C57

| RENTERS SKIP TO QUESTION 19. |

16. | Homeowners: | Have you participated in the
housing rehabilitation program?

  1 ___ Yes   2 ___ No   0 ___ Don't Know/No   16. ___
                                      Response   C58

17. | IF YES: | What kinds of services did you receive
from the rehabilitation program? (Can be more
than one.)

  a. 1 ___ Help finding a contractor   a. ___
                                                C59
  b. 2 ___ Help obtaining materials   b. ___
                                                C60
  c. 3 ___ Help with estimating costs   c. ___
                                                C61
  d. 4 ___ Rehabilitation grant from the city d. ___
                                                C62

e.   5 ___ Help getting a bank loan

                                               e.   ___

f.   6 ___ Help getting a rehabilitation loan
             from the city   C63

                                                f.   ___

g.   7 ___ Other (Please specify)_____

        _____   C64

                                                g.   ___

h.   0 ___ Don't Know/No Response   C65

                                              h.   ___

18. | IF NO: | Why didn't you participate? (Can be   C66
     more than one.)

          | OPEN ENDED. DO NOT READ RESPONSES. |

     1 ___ House was found to be in compliance   18. 1

     2 ___ I don't like the idea of welfare   2   C67

     3 ___ Too expensive   3   C68

     4 ___ I haven't gotten around to it   4   C69

     0 ___ Don't Know/No Response   0   C70

     5 ___ Other (Please specify) _____   C71

     _____

     _____   5 ___ ___
                                                    C72 C73

19. How many people are living in this household
     at present?

     _____   19.
                                                  C74 C75

20. How many are between ages 5 and 18? _____   20.
                                                    C76 C77

21. How many are children under 5 years old?

     _____   21.
                                                  C78 C79

22. In what year were you born? _____   22.
                                         C5 C6 C7

23. Card Number   23.
                                                  C1

24. Case Number   24.
                                      C2 C3 C4

25. How many are 65 years old or more? _____ 25.
                                                  C8 C9

26. How many members of this household regularly
     work outside the home 30 hours a week or
     more?   26.

                                                  C10 C11

27. What is your marital status?

     1 ___ Single   2 ___ Married

3 ___ Separated   4 ___ Divorced

5 ___ Widowed   27. ___
                                              C12

28. What is the highest grade you completed in
     school?

     0 ___ No Response   5 ___ Some College

     1 ___ No High School   6 ___ College Grad.

     2 ___ Some High School   7 ___ Some Grad.
                                    School
     3 ___ High School Grad.
                              8 ___ Master's Degree
     4 ___ Technical or
            Business School   9 ___ Doctor's Degree   28. ___
                                                          C13

29. How many licensed drivers are there in this
     household? _____   29. ___ ___
                                                    C14 C15

30. How many licensed, operable automobiles are
     owned by members of the household, including
     small trucks, used for family or individual
     trips? _____   30. ___ ___
                                                    C16 C17

31. In which of the following broad categories
     would your current annual family income fall?
     (Include all sources of income.)

     0 ___ No Response/Don't Know

     1 ___ $5,000 or less

     2 ___ $5,000 to $10,000

     3 ___ $10,000 to $15,000

     4 ___ $15,000 to $20,000

     5 ___ $20,000 to $25,000

     6 ___ $25,000 or More   31. ___
                                                    C18

Recap Sheet

Inspector's Initials				
Week Ending				

Address:_____

Owner:_____

1. Initial Inspection   Date_____

   A. Compliance_____
   B. Violation_____
   C. Refused Entry_____
   D. Could Not Contact_____
   E. Inspection Rescheduled_____   Date_____
   F. Entry Warrant Issued_____
   G. Recommended for Demo_____
   H. Board-Up_____
   I. Sanitation Violation_____
   J. Buyer Notification_____
   K. Rent Withholding_____

2. Occupancy Status

   A. Owner Occupied_____Mortgage_____
      Sales Agreement_____
   B. Tenant_____
   C. Vacant_____
   D. Number of Units in Structure_____

3. Work Write-Up

   A. In Progress_____
   B. Complete_____

4. Cost Estimate

   A. In Progress_____
   B. Complete_____
   C. Estimated Cost_____

5. Financial Counseling

   A. Type of Grant Applicable: 15% 25% 40% (circle one)
   B. Program Explained_____
   C. Owner Expressed Interest_____ No Interest_____
      Moderate Interest_____
   D. Schedule for Rehab Established_____

6. Reinspection   Date_____

   A. Brought into Compliance_____
   B. Started_____
   C. Not Started_____
   D. Sanitation Violations Corrected_____
      Not Corrected_____
   E. Could Not Contact_____   Date_____

7. Enforcement (Specify)

   A. Sanitation_____
   B. Code Enforcement_____

8. Contract Selection

   A. Owner will do Work_____
   B. Contractor will do Work_____

C. Contractor and Owner will do Work_____
D. Contractor Selection_____
    1) In Progress_____
        No. of bids: General___Elect.___Plumbing___
    2) Complete_____

9. Financing

    A. Application made to Bank_____   Date_____
        1) Approved (attach sheet indicating breakdown)_____
        2) Disapproved_____
        3) Referred to Loan Committee_____ Date_____
            a) Approved_____
            b) Disapproved_____
    B. Non-Loan Subsidy Recipient_____
        (attach sheet indicating breakdown)
    C. Non-Subsidy Recipient_____
    D. Loan Default_____ Loan Collection Started_____

10. Compliance Rehab

    A. Proceed Order Given_____   Date_____
    B. Work in Progress_____
    C. Work Inspected_____ Date_____ Date_____
    D. Work Completed_____
    E. Certificate Issued_____   Date_____
    F. Bank Issued Check (90% Payment)_____
    G. Structure in Total Compliance_____
    H. Structure in Partial Compliance_____
        1) What will be done to complete work?
        2) When_____

    I. Final Certificate Issued_____ Date_____
    J. Final Payment made to Contractor_____

11. Final Reinspections

    A. Dates_____   _____   _____

    Comments: (please initial)

Financial Tally Sheet

Repairs_____

Grant_____

City Share_____

Total Loan Amount_____

  Principal_____

  Interest_____

  Other (Specify)_____

  Term_____yrs.

Monthly Payment_____

   Date Due_____

10% Escrow_____

100% Escrow
   Plus Interest_____

Monthly Reporting Form: Site Offices

Emphasis Area_____Month of _____

1. Number of initial code inspections.   1._____

2. Number of structures found to be in violation
    of (non-sanitation) codes.   2._____

3. Number of sanitation violations.   3._____

4. Number of sanitation violations brought into
    compliance.   4._____

5. Total estimated cost of rehabilitation
    (structures identified in Item 2).   5._____

    Of those structures identified in Item 2:

    a. Number with rehabilitation costs below $500   a._____

    b. Number with rehabilitation costs ranging
        from $500 - $2500   b._____

    c. Number with rehabilitation costs ranging
        from $2500 - $5000   c._____

    d. Number with rehabilitation costs above
        $5000   d._____

6. Number of structures found to be in compliance. 6._____

7. Number of structures found to be unfit for
    rehabilitation.   7._____

8. Number of demolition permits issued.   8._____

9. Number of demolitions.   9._____

10. a. Number of new board-ups   10.a._____

    b. Number unboarded   b._____

11. Number refused entry for code inspection.   11._____

12.   Number of entry warrants issued.   12._____

13.   Number of property owners sent to District
      Justices (for non-compliance).   13._____

14.   Number of reinspections.   14._____

Perceptions and Evaluations of Housing, Public Services, and General Conditions in the Program and No-Program Neighborhoods

What do you think has happened to the market value of this property over the past three years?

	Whites						Nonwhites						Total					
	Program		No-Program		Total		Program		No-Program		Total		Program		No-Program		Total	
	Number	Percent	Number	Percent	Number	Percent	Number	Percent	Number	Percent	Number	Percent	Number	Percent	Number	Percent	Number	Percent
Increased	40	30.3	12	20.0	52	27.1	10	50.0	17	42.5	27	45.0	50	32.9	29	29.0	79	31.3
Decreased	52	39.4	28	46.7	80	41.7	6	30.0	8	20.0	14	23.3	58	38.2	36	36.0	94	37.3
Stayed about the same	40	30.3	20	33.3	60	31.3	4	20.0	15	37.5	19	31.7	44	28.9	35	35.0	79	31.3
Total	132	100.0	60	100.0	192	100.1	20	100.0	40	100.0	60	100.0	152	100.0	100	100.0	252	99.9

(Owners) Are you satisfied with your house in meeting your needs?

	Whites						Nonwhites						Total					
	Program		No-Program		Total		Program		No-Program		Total		Program		No-Program		Total	
	Number	Percent	Number	Percent	Number	Percent	Number	Percent	Number	Percent	Number	Percent	Number	Percent	Number	Percent	Number	Percent
Satisfied	126	92.0	61	95.3	187	93.0	15	75.0	34	87.2	49	83.1	141	89.8	95	92.2	236	90.8
Dissatisfied	11	8.0	3	4.7	14	7.0	5	25.0	5	12.8	10	16.9	16	10.2	8	7.8	24	9.2
Total	137	100.0	64	100.0	201	100.0	20	100.0	39	100.0	59	100.0	157	100.0	103	100.0	260	100.0

This neighborhood is a better place in which to live than it was two or three years ago.

	Whites						Nonwhites						Total					
	Program		No-Program		Total		Program		No-Program		Total		Program		No-Program		Total	
	Number	Percent	Number	Percent	Number	Percent	Number	Percent	Number	Percent	Number	Percent	Number	Percent	Number	Percent	Number	Percent
Disagree	131	78.4	67	80.7	198	79.2	17	53.1	37	66.1	54	61.4	148	74.4	104	74.8	252	74.6
Agree	36	21.6	16	19.3	52	20.8	15	46.9	19	33.9	34	38.6	51	25.6	35	25.2	86	25.4
Total	167	100.0	83	100.0	250	100.0	32	100.0	56	100.0	88	100.0	199	100.0	139	100.0	338	100.0

Over the past two or three years, the number of abandoned buildings in this neighborhood has increased.

	Whites						Nonwhites						Total					
	Program		No-Program		Total		Program		No-Program		Total		Program		No-Program		Total	
	Number	Percent	Number	Percent	Number	Percent	Number	Percent	Number	Percent	Number	Percent	Number	Percent	Number	Percent	Number	Percent
Agree	64	40.0	38	46.9	102	42.3	16	55.2	32	52.5	48	53.3	80	42.3	70	49.3	150	45.3
Disagree	96	60.0	43	53.1	139	57.7	13	44.8	29	47.5	42	46.7	109	57.7	72	50.7	181	54.7
Total	160	100.0	81	100.0	241	100.0	29	100.0	61	100.0	90	100.0	189	100.0	142	100.0	331	100.0

This neighborhood is visually attractive, as compared with other neighborhoods in the city.

	Whites						Nonwhites						Total					
	Program		No-Program		Total		Program		No-Program		Total		Program		No-Program		Total	
	Number	Percent	Number	Percent	Number	Percent	Number	Percent	Number	Percent	Number	Percent	Number	Percent	Number	Percent	Number	Percent
No	115	62.2	59	64.1	174	62.8	18	46.2	32	47.8	50	47.2	133	59.4	91	57.2	224	58.5
Yes	70	37.8	33	35.9	103	37.2	21	53.8	35	52.2	56	52.8	91	40.6	68	42.8	159	41.5
Total	185	100.0	92	100.0	277	100.0	39	100.0	67	100.0	106	100.0	224	100.0	159	100.0	383	100.0

The streets in this neighborhood are *not* well lighted at night.

	Whites						Nonwhites						Total					
	Program		No-Program		Total		Program		No-Program		Total		Program		No-Program		Total	
	Number	Percent	Number	Percent	Number	Percent	Number	Percent	Number	Percent	Number	Percent	Number	Percent	Number	Percent	Number	Percent
Agree	8	4.3	19	20.9	27	9.8	5	12.8	19	28.8	24	22.9	13	5.8	38	24.2	51	13.4
Disagree	176	95.7	72	79.1	248	90.2	34	87.2	47	71.2	81	77.1	210	94.2	119	75.8	329	86.6
Total	184	100.0	91	100.0	275	100.0	39	100.0	66	100.0	105	100.0	223	99.9	157	100.0	380	100.0

Abandoned houses and other empty buildings are a big problem in this neighborhood.

	Whites						Nonwhites						Total					
	Program		No-Program		Total		Program		No-Program		Total		Program		No-Program		Total	
	Number	Percent	Number	Percent	Number	Percent	Number	Percent	Number	Percent	Number	Percent	Number	Percent	Number	Percent	Number	Percent
Agree	69	38.3	41	47.1	110	41.2	14	37.8	35	53.0	49	47.6	83	38.2	76	49.7	159	43.0
Disagree	111	61.7	46	52.9	157	58.8	23	62.2	31	47.0	54	52.4	134	61.8	77	50.3	211	57.0
Total	180	100.0	87	100.0	267	100.0	37	100.0	66	100.0	103	100.0	217	100.0	153	100.0	370	100.0

Trash collection is poor in this neighborhood.

	Whites						Nonwhites						Total					
	Program		No-Program		Total		Program		No-Program		Total		Program		No-Program		Total	
	Number	Percent	Number	Percent	Number	Percent	Number	Percent	Number	Percent	Number	Percent	Number	Percent	Number	Percent	Number	Percent
Agree	21	11.5	14	15.2	35	12.7	6	15.4	12	18.2	18	17.1	27	12.2	26	16.5	53	13.9
Disagree	162	88.5	78	84.8	240	87.3	33	84.6	54	81.8	87	82.9	195	87.8	132	83.5	327	86.1
Total	183	100.0	92	100.0	275	100.0	39	100.0	66	100.0	105	100.0	222	100.0	158	100.0	380	100.0

Over the past two or three years housing conditions in this neighborhood have improved significantly.

	Whites						Nonwhites						Total					
	Program		No-Program		Total		Program		No-Program		Total		Program		No-Program		Total	
	Number	Percent	Number	Percent	Number	Percent	Number	Percent	Number	Percent	Number	Percent	Number	Percent	Number	Percent	Number	Percent
Disagree	100	60.6	59	67.8	159	63.1	18	58.1	40	66.7	58	63.7	118	60.2	99	67.3	217	63.3
Agree	65	39.4	28	32.2	93	36.9	13	41.9	20	33.3	33	36.3	78	39.8	48	32.7	126	36.7
Total	165	100.0	87	100.0	252	100.0	31	100.0	60	100.0	91	100.0	196	100.0	147	100.0	343	100.0

Police provide good service to this neighborhood.

	Whites						Nonwhites						Total					
	Program		No-Program		Total		Program		No-Program		Total		Program		No-Program		Total	
	Number	Percent	Number	Percent	Number	Percent	Number	Percent	Number	Percent	Number	Percent	Number	Percent	Number	Percent	Number	Percent
Disagree	48	27.3	30	34.9	78	29.8	6	16.2	27	42.2	33	32.7	54	25.4	57	38.0	111	30.6
Agree	128	72.7	56	65.1	184	70.2	31	83.8	37	57.8	68	67.3	159	74.6	93	62.0	252	69.4
Total	176	100.0	86	100.0	262	100.0	37	100.0	64	100.0	101	100.0	213	100.0	150	100.0	363	100.0

This neighborhood is a good place in which to bring up children.

	Whites						Nonwhites						Total					
	Program		No-Program		Total		Program		No-Program		Total		Program		No-Program		Total	
	Number	Percent	Number	Percent	Number	Percent	Number	Percent	Number	Percent	Number	Percent	Number	Percent	Number	Percent	Number	Percent
Disagree	124	75.2	58	69.9	182	73.4	16	43.2	23	36.5	39	39.0	140	69.3	81	55.5	221	63.5
Agree	41	24.8	25	30.1	66	26.6	21	56.8	40	63.5	61	61.0	62	30.7	65	44.5	127	36.5
Total	165	100.0	83	100.0	248	100.0	37	100.0	63	100.0	100	100.0	202	100.0	146	100.0	348	100.0

This neighborhood is deteriorating fast.

	Whites						Nonwhites						Total					
	Program		No-Program		Total		Program		No-Program		Total		Program		No-Program		Total	
	Number	Percent	Number	Percent	Number	Percent	Number	Percent	Number	Percent	Number	Percent	Number	Percent	Number	Percent	Number	Percent
Agree	126	70.4	61	71.8	187	70.8	22	61.1	27	44.3	49	50.5	148	68.8	88	60.3	236	65.4
Disagree	53	29.6	24	28.2	77	29.2	14	38.9	34	55.7	48	49.5	67	31.2	58	39.7	125	34.6
Total	179	100.0	85	100.0	264	100.0	36	100.0	61	100.0	97	100.0	215	100.0	146	100.0	361	100.0

The city government is committed to improving the quality of this neighborhood.

	Whites						Nonwhites						Total					
	Program		No-Program		Total		Program		No-Program		Total		Program		No-Program		Total	
	Number	Percent	Number	Percent	Number	Percent	Number	Percent	Number	Percent	Number	Percent	Number	Percent	Number	Percent	Number	Percent
Disagree	55	34.8	53	76.8	108	47.6	13	36.1	41	71.9	54	58.1	68	35.1	94	74.6	162	50.6
Agree	103	65.2	16	23.2	119	52.4	23	63.9	16	28.1	39	41.9	126	64.9	32	25.4	158	49.4
Total	158	100.0	69	100.0	227	100.0	36	100.0	57	100.0	93	100.0	194	100.0	126	100.0	320	100.0

People in this neighborhood are taking better care of their homes than they were two or three years ago.

	Whites						Nonwhites						Total					
	Program		No-Program		Total		Program		No-Program		Total		Program		No-Program		Total	
	Number	Percent	Number	Percent	Number	Percent	Number	Percent	Number	Percent	Number	Percent	Number	Percent	Number	Percent	Number	Percent
Disagree	80	49.7	47	56.0	127	51.8	13	41.9	22	40.0	35	40.7	93	48.4	69	49.6	162	48.9
Agree	81	50.3	37	44.0	118	48.2	18	58.1	33	60.0	51	59.3	99	51.6	70	50.4	169	51.1
Total	161	100.0	84	100.0	245	100.0	31	100.0	55	100.0	86	100.0	192	100.0	139	100.0	331	100.0

This neighborhood is served with good recreational facilities.

	Whites						Nonwhites						Total					
	Program		No-Program		Total		Program		No-Program		Total		Program		No-Program		Total	
	Number	Percent	Number	Percent	Number	Percent	Number	Percent	Number	Percent	Number	Percent	Number	Percent	Number	Percent	Number	Percent
Disagree	104	62.3	58	73.4	162	65.9	20	54.1	38	58.5	58	56.9	124	60.8	96	66.7	220	63.2
Agree	63	37.7	21	26.6	84	34.1	17	45.9	27	41.5	44	43.1	80	39.2	48	33.3	128	36.8
Total	167	100.0	79	100.0	246	100.0	37	100.0	65	100.0	102	100.0	204	100.0	144	100.0	348	100.0

A person is safe from crime in this neighborhood.

Whites

	Program		No-Program		Total	
	Number	Percent	Number	Percent	Number	Percent
Disagree	116	64.8	63	71.6	179	67.0
Agree	63	35.2	25	28.4	88	33.0
Total	179	100.0	88	100.0	267	100.0

Nonwhites

	Program		No-Program		Total	
	Number	Percent	Number	Percent	Number	Percent
Disagree	21	55.3	31	49.2	52	51.5
Agree	17	44.7	32	50.8	49	48.5
Total	38	100.0	63	100.0	101	100.0

Total

	Program		No-Program		Total	
	Number	Percent	Number	Percent	Number	Percent
Disagree	137	63.1	94	62.2	231	62.8
Agree	80	36.9	57	37.8	137	37.2
Total	217	100.0	151	100.0	368	100.0

Streets and sidewalks in this neighborhood are in good condition.

Whites

	Program		No-Program		Total	
	Number	Percent	Number	Percent	Number	Percent
Disagree	99	53.8	62	67.4	161	58.3
Agree	85	46.2	30	32.6	115	41.7
Total	184	100.0	92	100.0	276	100.0

Nonwhites

	Program		No-Program		Total	
	Number	Percent	Number	Percent	Number	Percent
Disagree	24	61.5	39	58.2	63	59.4
Agree	15	38.5	28	41.8	43	40.6
Total	39	100.0	67	100.0	106	100.0

Total

	Program		No-Program		Total	
	Number	Percent	Number	Percent	Number	Percent
Disagree	123	55.2	101	63.5	224	58.6
Agree	100	44.8	58	36.5	158	41.4
Total	223	100.0	159	100.0	382	100.0

Housing in this neighborhood is in good condition.

Whites

	Program		No-Program		Total	
	Number	Percent	Number	Percent	Number	Percent
Disagree	109	61.2	49	55.7	158	59.4
Agree	69	38.8	39	44.3	108	40.6
Total	178	100.0	88	100.0	266	100.0

Nonwhites

	Program		No-Program		Total	
	Number	Percent	Number	Percent	Number	Percent
Disagree	20	51.3	40	65.6	60	60.0
Agree	19	48.7	21	34.4	40	40.0
Total	39	100.0	61	100.0	100	100.0

Total

	Program		No-Program		Total	
	Number	Percent	Number	Percent	Number	Percent
Disagree	129	59.4	89	59.7	218	59.6
Agree	88	40.6	60	40.3	148	40.4
Total	217	100.0	149	100.0	366	100.0

This neighborhood is becoming a less desirable place in which to live.

Whites

	Program		No-Program		Total	
	Number	Percent	Number	Percent	Number	Percent
Agree	133	75.1	66	73.3	199	74.5
Disagree	44	24.9	24	26.7	68	25.5
Total	177	100.0	90	100.0	267	100.0

Nonwhites

	Program		No-Program		Total	
	Number	Percent	Number	Percent	Number	Percent
Agree	19	51.4	37	57.8	56	55.4
Disagree	18	48.6	27	42.2	45	44.6
Total	37	100.0	64	100.0	101	100.0

Total

	Program		No-Program		Total	
	Number	Percent	Number	Percent	Number	Percent
Agree	150	70.8	103	66.9	255	69.3
Disagree	62	29.2	51	33.1	113	30.7
Total	212	100.0	154	100.0	368	100.0

Over the past two or three years, crime in this neighborhood has increased.

Whites

	Program		No-Program		Total	
	Number	Percent	Number	Percent	Number	Percent
Agree	81	49.7	52	64.2	133	54.5
Disagree	82	50.3	29	35.8	111	45.5
Total	163	100.0	81	100.0	244	100.0

Nonwhites

	Program		No-Program		Total	
	Number	Percent	Number	Percent	Number	Percent
Agree	12	40.0	14	26.9	26	31.7
Disagree	18	60.0	38	73.1	56	68.3
Total	30	100.0	52	100.0	82	100.0

Total

	Program		No-Program		Total	
	Number	Percent	Number	Percent	Number	Percent
Agree	93	48.2	66	49.6	159	48.8
Disagree	100	51.8	67	50.4	167	51.2
Total	193	100.0	133	100.0	326	100.0

If you had a choice, would you prefer to stay in this neighborhood or move?

Whites

	Program		No-Program		Total	
	Number	Percent	Number	Percent	Number	Percent
Stay	87	47.0	46	50.0	133	48.0
Move	92	49.7	41	44.6	133	48.0
Don't Know/No Response	6	3.2	5	5.4	11	4.0
Total	185	100.0	92	100.0	277	100.0

Nonwhites

	Program		No-Program		Total	
	Number	Percent	Number	Percent	Number	Percent
Stay	22	56.4	45	67.2	67	63.2
Move	17	43.6	20	29.9	37	34.9
Don't Know/No Response	—	—	2	3.0	2	1.9
Total	39	100.0	67	100.0	106	100.0

Total

	Program		No-Program		Total	
	Number	Percent	Number	Percent	Number	Percent
Stay	109	48.6	91	57.2	200	52.2
Move	109	48.6	61	38.4	170	44.4
Don't Know/No Response	6	2.7	7	4.4	13	3.4
Total	224	100.0	159	100.0	383	100.0

Rating of public services in the neighborhood relative to the rest of the city:

Whites

	Program		No-Program		Total	
	Number	Percent	Number	Percent	Number	Percent
Better	34	21.1	12	14.3	46	18.8
Same	101	62.7	51	60.7	152	62.0
Not As Good	10	6.2	15	17.9	25	10.2
Uncertain	16	9.9	6	7.1	22	9.0
Total	161	99.9	84	100.0	245	100.0

Nonwhites

	Program		No-Program		Total	
	Number	Percent	Number	Percent	Number	Percent
Better	10	28.6	6	9.4	16	16.2
Same	19	54.3	48	75.0	67	67.7
Not As Good	4	11.4	9	14.1	13	13.1
Uncertain	2	5.7	1	1.6	3	3.0
Total	35	100.0	64	100.1	99	100.0

Total

	Program		No-Program		Total	
	Number	Percent	Number	Percent	Number	Percent
Better	44	22.1	18	12.1	62	17.8
Same	123	61.8	99	66.4	222	63.8
Not As Good	14	7.0	25	16.8	39	11.2
Uncertain	18	9.0	7	4.7	25	7.2
Total	199	99.9	149	100.0	348	100.0

Properties in this neighborhood are well maintained.

Whites

	Program		No-Program		Total	
	Number	Percent	Number	Percent	Number	Percent
Disagree	116	63.7	53	60.9	169	62.8
Agree	66	36.3	34	39.1	100	37.2
Total	182	100.0	87	100.0	269	100.0

Nonwhites

	Program		No-Program		Total	
	Number	Percent	Number	Percent	Number	Percent
Disagree	18	46.2	35	53.0	53	50.5
Agree	21	53.8	31	47.0	52	49.5
Total	39	100.0	66	100.0	105	100.0

Total

	Program		No-Program		Total	
	Number	Percent	Number	Percent	Number	Percent
Disagree	134	60.6	88	57.5	222	59.4
Agree	87	39.4	65	42.5	152	40.6
Total	221	100.0	153	100.0	374	100.0

Appendix C
Williamsport Area
Bus Rider Survey

_____Route _____Distributor

To Our Patrons: You can help the Williamsport Bureau of Transportation improve bus service by answering the
following questions. It is important that you
fill out a card for each time you ride the bus
today. If you have any questions, please ask
the person who is handing out the surveys.
Drop the completed card in the large container
by the bus door.

A. Please fill in the specific time you boarded this bus.
_____AM or _____PM

B. Where did you start this trip?
(Give address or nearest intersecting streets)_____

_____

This is in:

Do not fill in Box

☐ 1. Williamsport   OX_____

☐ 2. Montoursville   OY_____

☐ 3. Old Lycoming Township

☐ 4. Loyalsock Township

☐ 5. South Williamsport

☐ 6. Duboistown

C. Where are you coming from:

☐ 1. Home   ☐ 4. Shopping

☐ 2. Work   ☐ 5. Doctor/Medical

☐ 3. School/   ☐ 6. Social Service Agency
       College
                    ☐ 7. Other

D. How far did you walk to the bus stop?
_____Blocks   _____Did not walk

E. Where are you going?
    (Give address or nearest intersecting streets)_____

	Do not fill in box
This destination is in:	
☐ 1. Williamsport	DX_____
☐ 2. Montoursville	DY_____
☐ 3. Old Lycoming Township	
☐ 4. Loyalsock Township	
☐ 5. South Williamsport	
☐ 6. Duboistown	

F. The place you are going to is:

    ☐ 1. Home   ☐ 4. Shopping

    ☐ 2. Work   ☐ 5. Doctor/Medical

    ☐ 3. School/   ☐ 6. Social Service Agency
          College
                            ☐ 7. Other

G. Will you have to transfer to another bus to complete your one
    way trip?
                 ☐ 1. Yes ☐ 2. No   If yes, to what line?
                                       _____

H. About how far will you have to walk to your destination after
    you get off the bus? _____blocks

         If you have filled out this questionnaire before, skip
         the remaining questions. If not, please continue.

I. What are the primary reasons you ride the bus. (Check up to
    two)

    ☐ 1. Parking difficult   ☐ 4. No Driver's License

    ☐ 2. No Auto Available   ☐ 5. Free Fare for Senior
                                       Citizens
    ☐ 3. Prefer the Bus
                                 ☐ 6. Other (Please specify)
                                       _____

J. How do you rate the following aspects of the present bus
    service?

	Poor	Fair	Good	Very Good	Don't Know
Frequency of Buses	☐	☐	☐	☐	☐
Convenience of Transfers	☐	☐	☐	☐	☐
Schedule Reliability	☐	☐	☐	☐	☐
Condition of Buses	☐	☐	☐	☐	☐
Driver Competence	☐	☐	☐	☐	☐
Driver Courtesy	☐	☐	☐	☐	☐
Fares	☐	☐	☐	☐	☐
Areas Covered by Routes	☐	☐	☐	☐	☐

K. Check up to three of the bus improvements listed below which
    you would recommend. If you would recommend more than 3,
    check the 3 you think are most important.

    ☐ 1. Routes closer to home or destination

    ☐ 2. Benches or shelters at bus stops

    ☐ 3. New air-conditioned buses

    ☐ 4. More frequent rush hour service

    ☐ 5. Use of annual or 6 month passes

    ☐ 6. Arrive and depart on schedule

    ☐ 7. Better schedule and route information

    ☐ 8. Sunday service

    ☐ 9. More evening service

    ☐ 10. Easier transfers

    ☐ 11. Lower steps on buses

    ☐ 12. Easier route identification

    ☐ 13. Other (Specify)_____

L. How many cars in operating condition are there in your house-
    hold?

    ☐ 1. None   ☐ 3. Two cars

☐ 2. One car   ☐ 4. Three or more cars

M. Your Sex: ☐ 1. Female   ☐ 2. Male

N. To what age group do you belong?

    ☐ 1. 13 or under   ☐ 4. 25 to 44

    ☐ 2. 14 to 18   ☐ 5. 45 to 64

    ☐ 3. 19 to 24   ☐ 6. 65 or over

O. In which of the following ranges does your annual family
income fall?

    ☐ 1. Less than $3,000   ☐ 4. $10,000 - $15,000

    ☐ 2. $3,000 - $6,000   ☐ 5. Over $15,000

    ☐ 3. $6,000 - $10,000   ☐ 6. Don't know

Please use this space for any comments or suggestions you wish to
make. Thank you for your cooperation.

WILLIAMSPORT BUREAU OF TRANSPORTATION

Appendix D
City of York
Burglary-Prevention
Program Evaluation
Survey (Telephone)

1. First, I'm going to read you a list. Would you please tell me which of these things people in your neighborhood have done since Neighborhood Watch was organized that they had not done before? (Check only those things indicated as having been done.)

    Have they:

    _____ locked windows and doors?

    _____ installed locks and/or bars on windows or doors?

    _____ made it appear as though someone were home when they are away? (left lights on, etc.)

    _____ installed outside lighting?

    _____ installed a burglar alarm?

    _____ acquired a dog?

    _____ marked valuables with an identification number?

    _____ acquired a weapon?

    _____ acquired a freon horn?

    _____ paid attention to what goes on around their neighbors homes and joined in neighborhood cooperation?

    _____ anything else? _____

2. Have peoples' attitudes toward crime reporting been affected by the Neighborhood Watch Program?

    _____ YES   _____ NO

    a. If yes: How? _____

    _____

3. What percentage of the people on your block have become involved in the Neighborhood Watch Program?

    _____ percent

4. How many meetings have been held on your block since the block was organized? (excluding organizational meetings)

   _____

5. What is the average number of people attending these meetings?

   _____

6. What proportion of the people living on your block attend these meetings?

   _____

7. How can the Home Security Survey be promoted more effectively?

   _____

   _____

   a. Why are people so reluctant about this public service?

      _____

      _____

8. What problems have you encountered in soliciting cooperation from the people on your block?

   _____

   _____

9. What suggestions do you have to make the Neighborhood Watch Program more effective; that is, more likely to reduce crimes committed?

   _____

   _____

Index

Index

About the Authors

Theodore H. Poister, assistant professor of public administration at The Pennsylvania State University, received the M.P.A. degree and the Ph.D. in social science from the Maxwell School of Syracuse University. He has taught previously at Southern University in Baton Rouge, Louisiana, and served as a city planner with the Peace Corps in Chile. His principal teaching and research interests lie in the area of public policy analysis and urban management, with an additional specialization in transportation planning and policy. He has contributed articles to various social science and transportation journals and is the author of a recent text entitled *Public Program Analysis: Applied Research Methods* (Baltimore: University Park Press, 1978). Dr. Poister has also served as a consultant with several state and local agencies.

James C. McDavid is a faculty member at the Institute of Public Administration, The Pennsylvania State University, University Park Campus. His interest in program evaluation has developed through research, teaching, and consulting work he has done while at Penn State. He also has active interests in research related to criminal justice administration, urban administration, and intergovernmental relations. He has published articles in *Publius, Journal of Criminal Justice, Police Chief*, and the *International Journal of Public Administration*. The Pennsylvania State Press is publishing his book, *Police Cooperation and Performance: The Greater St. Louis Interlocal Experience*.

Anne Hoagland Magoun attended Smith College and was graduated from Yale University. She received the master of public administration degree from The Pennsylvania State University and was employed as a research assistant at the Institute of Public Administration when she participated on the Harrisburg Housing Rehabilitation program. She presently lives in North Haven, Connecticut.